History Foretold:
The Book of Daniel

liegengelassen, obwohl es da halbnackt erfrieren hätte können, und seien unter höhnischem Gelächter davongerast.

Seit dem Wegfall des Eisernen Vorhangs, der nach dem Zweiten Weltkrieg Deutschland und Europa trennte, und der damit erfolgten Öffnung der Grenze zum Osten schlichen sich über die Grüne Grenze viele Burschen und Männer verschiedenster Nationen ein, die hier Verbrechen begingen, sich der Festnahme entzogen und stehenden Fußes über die Grenze sich absetzten.

Um sich die Last vom Herzen zu nehmen, schrieb Sophie ihrer Mutter einen Brief, in dem sie ihre Ängste und Träume darlegte. Die Mama antwortete liebevoll und tröstete ihre Tochter, indem sie ihr versicherte, daß sie allzeit für sie beten werde. Und wenn nichts mehr helfe, beten helfe immer. So ließ sich die Tochter beruhigen.

Die Tage vergingen, die Arbeit der Ärztin wurde immer umfangreicher. Sie hatte keine Zeit, den Gedanken und Befürchtungen nachzugehen.

VII.

Tage und Nächte wechselten sich ab, Wochen und Monate gingen übers Land. Bei der Sophie häufte sich die Arbeit. An Dienstagen und Freitagen blieb sie bis 8 Uhr oder 9 Uhr nachts in der Praxis, oft auch länger, bis sie den letzten Patienten untersucht und versorgt hatte.

Da wurde sie eines Tages, als es schon finster geworden war und eine dichte Wolkendecke den Himmel verfinsterte, zur Oberloherin gerufen. Sie ringe nach Luft, drohe zu ersticken und werde von Stichschmerzen in der Brust geplagt.

Sophie packte in aller Eile den Notkoffer, bestieg das Auto und fuhr nach Oberlohe. Nach einem Kilometer versperrte ein rot-weißer Querbalken die Straße. Aufblinkende Warnlampen sicherten die Sperre. Ein rundes weißes Schild mit roter Umrandung besagte „Durchfahrt verboten".

Ohne den Grund der Absperrung zu kennen, nahm sie einen weiten Umweg, um zur Patientin zu gelangen. Dieser Umweg war ihr unbekannt. Er führte durch einsame Waldungen und lag abseits der bewohnten Dörfer und Weiler. Wegweiser waren nicht angebracht, da die dortige Gemeindeverwaltung, sorglos wie sie war, es vernachlässigt hatte, solche aufzustellen.

Während der Fahrt wuchs der Ostwind zu einem Orkan an und bog die Fichten und Tannen so stark, daß sie sich ächzend und knirschend halb zu Boden neigten. Die Sträucher und Gebüsche waren wie lebendige Geister, die hin und her huschten, miteinander mauschelten und wisperten. Es schien, als würden sie von Ort zu Ort schweben. Gut, daß hie und da ein Blitz das Firmament erleuchtete und Sophie wieder Orientierung fand. Der Platzregen prasselte auf die Straße nieder. Es bildeten sich Pfützen und Lachen.

Als sie an eine Weggabelung ankam, wo zwei schmale Pfade getrennt weiterführten, aber kein Zeichen Richtung und Ort angab, bog Sophie schnell entschlossen auf den rechten Weg ein, hoffend, auf ihm so rasch wie möglich nach Oberlohe zu gelangen. Sie mußte alle Aufmerksamkeit aufwenden, um mit dem VW Käfer, der sich sonst als recht geländegängig erwies, in der Spur zu bleiben und nicht in einen der links und rechts des Weges verlaufenden Gräben abzurutschen.

Da schimmerte zwischen den Baumstämmen von weit her ein Licht hindurch. Sophie war nun froh, bald, wie sie dachte, am Ziel in Oberlohe zu sein und atmete erleichtert auf. Sie hörte ihren eigenen Atem. Das gab ihr Hoffnung. Erst bog der Weg durch einen Jungwald. Die grünen Zweige ragten bis an die Fahrspur heran, und sie mußte auf den ersten Gang zurückschalten, um das Auto in diesem Wirrwar noch unter Kontrolle zu halten. Verkrampft umfaßte sie das Lenkrad. Dann erleicherte ein Hochwald die Fahrt. Die astlosten Stämme ließen einen weiten Blick auf die kommende Strecke zu. Der nächtliche Sturm raste über die Wipfel hinweg. Am Waldboden war nichts zu spüren.

Die Ärztin näherte sich merklich dem vorher wahrgenommenen Licht. Ein Holzlust von etwa fünf Meter hohen Fichten trennte sie noch vom erhofften Ziel.

Plötzlich lag ein Baumstamm quer über dem Weg. Sie mußte anhalten. Ihre Hände zitterten. Das Blut stockte ihr in den Adern. Da sprangen links und rechts aus dem Unterholz vermummte Burschen, die Pistolen drohend in den Händen hielten und sie auf die Ärztin richteten. Einige blieben im Schutz der Zweige verborgen und bewegten gespensterhaft die Zweige.

100

Introduction

Secular scholars claim the Bible could not possibly be true because many of the people mentioned have not been found in history. I find this a rather arrogant position to take since we are constantly discovering new information through archeology. More than once, secular historians have declared part of that Bible absolutely untrue ("David never existed. He is just a fable!") only to be proven wrong shortly thereafter ("Oh, gee. Here is a signet ring that clearly says it belonged to 'the son of King David of Israel.' Ooops.") This has happened often enough for me to think God is purposely making fools of modern historians; withholding evidence just long enough for them to publicly declare the Bible untrue, then, Wham! There's the proof it is true.

Even those who believe the Bible to be true sometimes have trouble, though. Part of the problem with correlating History with the Bible is that it was the norm for kings to have several names; the one mommy gave them, the one daddy gave them, the one their friends called them, the one their subjects called them, the one(s) their enemies called them. Since any one of these names may be used in any given historical record, sometimes it is hard to tell just how many different kings we are talking about.

And just to complicate things, many of our historical records come from the Greeks who translated the names they ran across into their own language. So in the Bible itself we may read the Hebrew, Arabic or Chaldean name for a person (or all three in different passages), but in history texts the person is called by their Greek name.

This especially complicates things in Daniel in regards to "Darius the Mede." Now, we know he wasn't

"Darius the Great" The famous Darius in history that fought with Greece came after Cyrus the Great. He is known as "Darius the Persian," not "Mede." So just who was "The Mede?" None of the Greek historians mention any such person.

However, recent research into Jewish and Persian records of the time (some just recently discovered) might clear things up a bit. Seems the Persians knew their own history better than the Greeks did. "Darius the Mede," for example, was probably "Cyrus the Great's" uncle/father-in-law who co-ruled in the very beginning of his empire.

The point is, we need to be clear in our beliefs. The Bible is absolutely true and reliable. If history appears to disagree with it, we just haven't discovered all the historical evidence yet. Time will reveal what we need to prove the validity of the Bible. We just need to have faith…and patience.

Chapter 1
DANIEL AND HIS FRIENDS STAND FIRM.

1 In the third year of the reign of Jehoiakim king of Judah, came Nebuchadnezzar king of Babylon unto Jerusalem, and besieged it.

The third year of Jehoiakim was the first or second year of Nebuchadnezzar, around 526_{BC} (about 3520 after Creation).

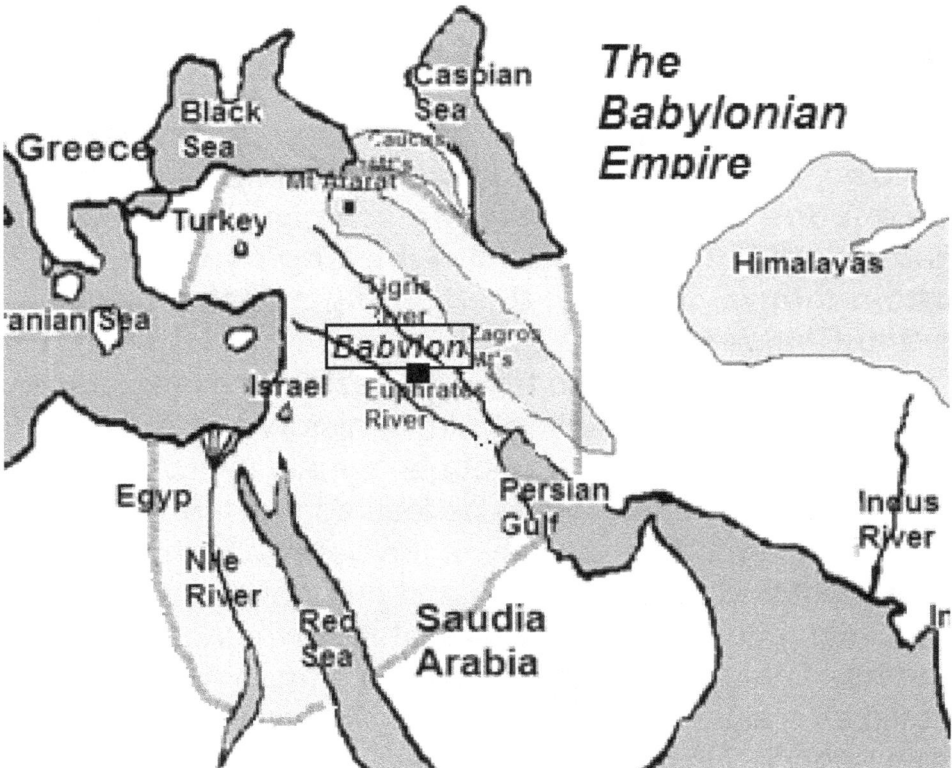

2 And the Lord gave Jehoiakim king of Judah into his hand, with part of the vessels of the house of God: which he carried into the land of Shinar to the

house of his god; and he brought the vessels into the treasure house of his god.

God is in control of all that happens. He allowed this foreign king to conquer Judah to punish them for their disobedience.

The land of Shinar is the area between the Tigris and Euphrates rivers. This area is also known as Mesopotamia, Sumer, and the Fertile Crescent.

3 And the king spake unto Ashpenaz the master of his eunuchs, that he should bring certain of the children of Israel, and of the king's seed, and of the princes;

4 Children in whom was no blemish, but well-favored, and skillful in all wisdom, and cunning in knowledge, and understanding science, and such as had ability in them to stand in the king's palace, and whom they might teach the learning and the tongue of the Chaldeans.

The king wanted to take the best young men of the land to work for him. At this point in history it was common for conquerors to both take male captives and castrate them so they would be less aggressive slaves or to take children of the royalty of the defeated land and treat them well, educate them and prepare them to rule in the assumption that they would return to their homeland and rule favorably for their conquerors (meanwhile they would also act as hostages keeping the conquered land from attacking in order to keep their children safe). We don't really know which was the motivation for Daniel's captivity.

We do know he was highly intelligent and received a high level education from his captors.

5 And the king appointed them a daily provision of the king's meat and of the wine which he drank: so nourishing them three years, that at the end thereof they might stand before the king.

The Bible doesn't tell us how old these young men were, but they were most likely in their teens. In America in the 1800's it was common for boys as young as fourteen to enter college. That is essentially the education Daniel now receives; a college degree.

6 Now among these were of the children of Judah; Daniel, Hananiah, Mishael, and Azariah:

7 Unto whom the prince of the eunuchs gave names: for he gave unto Daniel the name of Belteshazzar; and to Hananiah, of Shadrach; and to Mishael, of Meshach; and to Azariah, of Abednego.

Men by the names of Daniel, Hananiah, Mishael and Azariah are listed in the book of Ezra as returnees from Babylon around seventy years later. It is possible they are the same men.

8 But Daniel purposed in his heart that he would not defile himself with the portion of the king's meat, nor with the wine which he drank: therefore he requested of the prince of the eunuchs that he might not defile himself.

The king's food mentioned here was food commonly offered to idols before being eaten by the people. Since there is no prohibition in the Bible for eating either meat or drinking wine (though alcoholism is forbidden), we can assume that Daniel's objection to the king's food was the connection to the idols. Vegetables were not offered as often, being considered vulgar peasant food.

9 Now God had brought Daniel into favor and tender love with the prince of the eunuchs.

10 And the prince of the eunuchs said unto Daniel, "I fear my lord the king, who hath appointed your meat and your drink: for why should he see your faces worse liking than the children which are of your sort? Then shall ye make me endanger my head to the king?"

The common belief was that meat and wine was necessary for optimum health. Today we know that those who become vegetarians have a significant increase in overall health in the short-term, though in the long term they often suffer more cancers and anemia.

Tea-totalers have lower cancer rates than drinkers do. Most health benefits from drinking wine are easily obtainable from grape juice and other sources without the negative side effects of alcohol. If someone chooses to drink, it should be with moderation.

11 Then said Daniel to Melzar, whom the prince of the eunuchs had set over Daniel, Hananiah, Mishael, and Azariah,

12 "Prove thy servants, I beseech thee, ten days; and let them give us pulse to eat, and water to drink.

13 "Then let our countenances be looked upon before thee, and the countenance of the children that eat of the portion of the king's meat: and as thou seest, deal with thy servants."

14 So he consented to them in this matter, and proved them ten days.

15 And at the end of ten days their countenances appeared fairer and fatter in flesh than

all the children which did eat the portion of the king's meat.

There are a couple of explanations for this; the known short term effects of a vegetarian diet, less digestive trouble from a possibly radical change in diet, and Divine intervention. It was probably a combination of all three.

16 Thus Melzar took away the portion of their meat, and the wine that they should drink; and gave them pulse.

17 As for these four children, God gave them knowledge and skill in all learning and wisdom: and Daniel had understanding in all visions and dreams.

Here it tells us outright that God gave special gifts to Daniel and his friends. He had plans for them and equipped them to carry them out.

God will always give us whatever we need to accomplish His will in our lives. That may be money, but probably isn't. It is the talents and opportunities we need to follow Him.

18 Now at the end of the days that the king had said he should bring them in, then the prince of the eunuchs brought them in before Nebuchadnezzar.

19 And the king communed with them; and among them all was found none like Daniel, Hananiah, Mishael, and Azariah: therefore stood they before the king.

They were selected to work closely with the king-closer than anyone else.

20 And in all matters of wisdom and understanding, that the king enquired of them, he found them ten times better than all the magicians and astrologers that were in all his realm.

21 And Daniel continued even unto the first year of king Cyrus.

Daniel served the kings of Babylon until there were no more kings of Babylon.

Chapter 2
THE DREAM OF THE GREAT IDOL

1 And in the second year of the reign of Nebuchadnezzar, Nebuchadnezzar dreamed dreams, wherewith his spirit was troubled, and his sleep brake from him.

Ever had a dream like this? I sure have.

This was about 524$_{BC}$.

2 Then the king commanded to call the magicians, and the astrologers, and the sorcerers, and the Chaldeans, for to show the king his dreams. So they came and stood before the king.

3 And the king said unto them, "I have dreamed a dream, and my spirit was troubled to know the dream."

God often communicates with us through dreams. More often dreams simply mean we ate too much pizza before going to sleep, but it does happen for Him to speak to us in this way. I occasionally wake up having had a dream about someone I haven't thought of in years. I have discovered that this is God's way of telling me they need prayer.

Nebuchadnezzar knew this dream had something important to tell him.

4 Then spake the Chaldeans to the king in Syriack, "O king, live forever: tell thy servants the dream, and we will show the interpretation."

5 The king answered and said to the Chaldeans, "The thing is gone from me: if ye will not make known unto me the dream, with the interpretation thereof, ye shall be cut in pieces, and your houses shall be made a dunghill.

11

6 "But if ye show the dream, and the interpretation thereof, ye shall receive of me gifts and rewards and great honor: therefore show me the dream, and the interpretation thereof."

Talk about an impossible command! The king wanted them to tell him his dream and the interpretation... upon penalty of death, no less!

7 They answered again and said, "Let the king tell his servants the dream, and we will show the interpretation of it."

These men were the highest educated people in the kingdom and they made their living advising the king. They often used "magic" and superstition.

8 The king answered and said, "I know of certainty that ye would gain the time, because ye see the thing is gone from me."

"You're stalling!"

9 "But if ye will not make known unto me the dream, there is but one decree for you: for ye have prepared lying and corrupt words to speak before me, till the time be changed: therefore tell me the dream, and I shall know that ye can show me the interpretation thereof."

The king knew that they would lie to Him in order to save their lives, so he would accept nothing but the whole dream.

10 The Chaldeans answered before the king, and said, "There is not a man upon the earth that can show the king's matter: therefore there is no king, lord, nor ruler, that asked such things at any magician, or astrologer, or Chaldean.

11 "And it is a rare thing that the king requireth, and there is none other that can show it before the king, except the gods, whose dwelling is not with flesh."

"It's impossible!"

12 For this cause the king was angry and very furious, and commanded to destroy all the wise men of Babylon.

13 And the decree went forth that the wise men should be slain; and they sought Daniel and his fellows to be slain.

14 Then Daniel answered with counsel and wisdom to Arioch the captain of the king's guard, which was gone forth to slay the wise men of Babylon:

15 He answered and said to Arioch the king's captain, "Why is the decree so hasty from the king?" Then Arioch made the thing known to Daniel.

Evidently Daniel had not been called to the king when the other wise men were, though he was counted enough as one of them to be executed with them.

16 Then Daniel went in, and desired of the king that he would give him time, and that he would show the king the interpretation.

Daniel didn't tell the king he had asked an impossibility. He simply asked for a little time to pray about it. The king agreed.

17 Then Daniel went to his house, and made the thing known to Hananiah, Mishael, and Azariah, his companions:

18 That they would desire mercies of the God of heaven concerning this secret; that Daniel and his fellows should not perish with the rest of the wise men of Babylon.

They prayed. God always has His people in His hand and He guided Daniel. Prayer should always be our first action.

19 Then was the secret revealed unto Daniel in a night vision. Then Daniel blessed the God of heaven.

God told Daniel the king's dream in a dream of his own.

20 Daniel answered and said, "Blessed be the name of God for ever Daniel recognized the Hand of God and His greatness and guidance.

24 Therefore Daniel went in unto Arioch, whom the king had ordained to destroy the wise men of Babylon: he went and said thus unto him; "Destroy not the wise men of Babylon: bring me in before the king, and I will show unto the king the interpretation."

Daniel not only preserved his own life and the lives of his friends, he asked for the lives of the other wise men also. This shows true godly love.

25 Then Arioch brought in Daniel before the king in haste, and said thus unto him, "I have found a man of the captives of Judah, that will make known unto the king the interpretation."

26 The king answered and said to Daniel, whose name was Belteshazzar, "Art thou able to make known unto me the dream which I have seen, and the interpretation thereof?"

27 Daniel answered in the presence of the king, and said, "The secret which the king hath demanded cannot the wise men, the astrologers, the magicians, the soothsayers, show unto the king;

It is impossible for human beings to know another person's dream, no matter how smart they are.

28 "But there is a God in heaven that revealeth secrets, and maketh known to the king Nebuchadnezzar what shall be in the latter days...

Here Daniel introduces Nebuchadnezzar to the one true God. This may well have been Nebuchadnezzar's first knowledge of Him.

... Thy dream, and the visions of thy head upon thy bed, are these;

29 "As for thee, O king, thy thoughts came into thy mind upon thy bed, what should come to pass hereafter: and He that revealeth secrets maketh known to thee what shall come to pass.

"As you were going to sleep, you were wondering what will happen after you die. God decided to tell you."

30 "But as for me, this secret is not revealed to me for any wisdom that I have more than any living, but for their sakes that shall make known the interpretation to the king, and that thou mightest know the thoughts of thy heart.

"God didn't give me this answer because I am smarter or in any way better than anyone else. God gave me the answer because He wanted you to know."

The prophets of old always directed people away from themselves and towards God.

31 "You looked, O king, and there before you stood a large statue- an enormous, dazzling statue, awesome in appearance.

Beginning here, I will put the interpretation of the dreams immediately after the dream but in a different font.

36 This was the dream, and now we will interpret it to the king.

32 "The head of the statue was made of pure gold, ...

37 "You, O king, are the king of kings. That God of heaven has given you dominion and power and might and glory;

38 "In your hands He has placed mankind and the beasts of the field and the birds of the air. Wherever they live, He has made you ruler over them all. You are that head of gold.

This dream would have been about 524 $_{BC}$.

Gold was very common in Babylon at this time and the people had a very high standard of living.

...Its chest and arms of silver,

39 After you, another kingdom will rise, inferior to yours.

Medo/Persia. The Medes are building their army at this moment in history. (Cyrus conquers Babylon in 459 $_{BC}$). Silver was the currency in Persia. Taxes paid in gold were even converted to silver.

...Its belly and thighs of bronze,

...Next, a third kingdom, one of bronze, will rule over the whole earth.

Alexander the Great. At the time of this prophecy, Greece is nothing but a bunch of unconnected city-states. (Alexander died in 323 BC). Greece was the first army to use almost exclusively bronze shields and helmets.

33 Its legs of iron ...

40 Finally, there will be a fourth kingdom, strong as iron- for iron breaks and smashes everything- and

as iron breaks things to pieces, so it will crush and break all the others.

This is a history of the region of Babylon after Nebuchadnezzar. It would not be a very good history to leave out the entire Syrian empire. After the death of Alexander, Egypt took control of Israel, but Her king, Ptolemy, gave the northern part of his territory to his general, Seleucid, who ended up with the area of Babylon through Israel. His capital was in the country of Syria and his empire was known either by the name. "The Syrian Empire" or "The Seleucid Empire" and began somewhere between 323 and 310 BC). Syria used iron weapons.

Greece at the time of the Syrian Empire is just a small country with no control or influence over this region. It is fighting for its life with Rome and the countries to the north and east (Thrace, the fourth part of Alexander's kingdom.)

Rome is a republic, not an empire, and is also fighting for its life at the time of the Syrian empire, though its influence is growing.

...Its feet partly of iron and partly of baked clay.

41 "Just as you saw that the feet and toes were partly of baked clay and partly of iron, so this will be a divided kingdom; yet it will have some of the strength of iron in it, even as you saw iron mixed with clay.

42 "As the toes were partly of baked clay and partly of iron, so this will be partly strong and partly brittle.

43 "And just as you saw the iron mixed with baked clay, so the people will be a mixture and will

not remain united, any more than iron mixes with clay.

This is a perfect description of the Roman Empire, which began with Julius Caesar in 46 _{BC} and was the next major power in the Babylonian and Israelite regions. It was partly strong and partly weak, always had trouble controlling its very mixed people, constantly had to fight off the Gauls and other invaders from the north, had a system of appeals and allowed each people to govern itself and worship its own gods.

Rome also used iron weapons.

34 "While you were watching, a rock was cut out, but not by human hands. It struck the statue on its feet of iron and clay and smashed them.

35 Then the iron, the clay, the bronze, the silver and the gold were broken to pieces at the same time and became like chaff on a threshing floor in the summer. The wind swept them away without leaving a trace. But the rock that struck the statue became a huge mountain and filled the whole earth.

44 "In the time of those kings, (the kings of the final kingdom of clay and iron, Rome) the God of heaven will set up a kingdom that will never be destroyed, nor will it be left to another people. It will crush all those kingdoms and bring them to an end, but it will itself endure forever.

45 "This is the meaning of the vision of the Rock cut out of a mountain, but not by human hands- a Rock that broke the iron, the bronze, the clay, the silver and the gold to pieces. The Great God has shown the king what will take place in the future. The dream is true and the interpretation is trustworthy."

The Rock that crushed the whole thing by landing on the feet was Jesus and the church. The countries listed here are the nations that controlled God's church from Daniel until Christ. After The Cross, no political government was able to contain or control God's church. It grew to fill the whole planet. No longer could God's people be confined to one nation, one locality. The Kingdom of God will never end.

Paul tells us that God continues to put politicians into power and that He brings up and destroys kingdoms. God does still deal with nations, as our own history tells us. But His people are no longer identified by or confined to one nation or one country.

46 Then the king Nebuchadnezzar fell upon his face, and worshipped Daniel, and commanded that they should offer an oblation and sweet odors unto him.

47 The king answered unto Daniel, and said, "Of a truth it is, that your God is a God of gods, and a Lord of kings, and a revealer of secrets, seeing thou couldest reveal this secret."

The king was impressed. He believes in the power of Daniel's God, but has not yet accepted Him as his own God.

48 Then the king made Daniel a great man, and gave him many great gifts, and made him ruler over the whole province of Babylon, and chief of the governors over all the wise men of Babylon.

49 Then Daniel requested of the king, and he set Shadrach, Meshach, and Abednego, over the affairs of the province of Babylon: but Daniel sat in the gate of the king.

2. The Dream of the Great Idol

Daniel's friends were given important jobs, but Daniel became one of the chief rulers in the nation.

Chapter 3
THE FIERY FURNACE

We don't know where Daniel is during this story. There is no mention made of him one way or another. Some have speculated that he was away on business or that his high rank protected him, but it is just that, speculation.

1 Nebuchadnezzar the king made an image of gold, whose height was threescore cubits, and the breadth thereof six cubits: he set it up in the plain of Dura, in the province of Babylon.

We don't know what this image looked like. It could have been an image of Nebuchadnezzar, or just a plain obelisk or anything in between. The height may have included a pedestal.

2 Then Nebuchadnezzar the king sent to gather together the princes, the governors, and the captains, the judges, the treasurers, the counselors, the sheriffs, and all the rulers of the provinces, to come to the dedication of the image which Nebuchadnezzar the king had set up.

3 Then the princes, the governors, and the captains, the judges, the treasurers, the counselors, the sheriffs, and all the rulers of the provinces, were gathered together unto the dedication of the image that Nebuchadnezzar the king had set up; and they stood before the image that Nebuchadnezzar had set up.

4 Then a herald cried aloud, "To you it is commanded, O people, nations, and languages,

5 "That at what time ye hear the sound of the cornet, flute, harp, sackbut, psaltery, dulcimer, and all kinds of music, ye fall down and worship the golden image that Nebuchadnezzar the king hath set up:

Cornet, flute, harp, dulcimer are all instruments that are still common today. A sackbut is similar to a trombone. A psaltery is from the zither family, a type of lap harp.

6 "And whoso falleth not down and worshipeth shall the same hour be cast into the midst of a burning fiery furnace."

This was a serious threat for those who refuse the kings new god. He didn't tell them they had to give up their old gods, just add his to them.

7 Therefore at that time, when all the people heard the sound of the cornet, flute, harp, sackbut, psaltery, and all kinds of music, all the people, the nations, and the languages, fell down and worshipped the golden image that Nebuchadnezzar the king had set up.

Everyone obeyed the king.

8 Wherefore at that time certain Chaldeans came near, and accused the Jews.

9 They spake and said to the king "Nebuchadnezzar, O king, live forever.

10 "Thou, O king, hast made a decree, that every man that shall hear the sound of the cornet, flute, harp, sackbut, psaltery, and dulcimer, and all kinds of music, shall fall down and worship the golden image:

11 "And whoso falleth not down and worshipeth, that he should be cast into the midst of a burning fiery furnace.

12 "There are certain Jews whom thou hast set over the affairs of the province of Babylon, Shadrach,

Meshah, and Abednego; these men, O king, have not regarded thee: they serve not thy gods, nor worship the golden image which thou hast set up."

These men were most likely tattling out of jealousy, not devotion to the king and his idol.

13 Then Nebuchadnezzar in his rage and fury commanded to bring Shadrach, Meshach, and Abednego. Then they brought these men before the king.

14 Nebuchadnezzar spake and said unto them, "Is it true O Shadrach, Meshach, and

Abednego, do not ye serve my gods, nor worship the golden image which I have set up?

15 "Now if ye be ready that at what time ye hear the sound of the cornet, flute, harp, sackbut, psaltery, and dulcimer, and all kinds of music, ye fall down and worship the image which I have made; well: but if ye worship not, ye shall be cast the same hour into the midst of a burning fiery furnace; and who is that god that shall deliver you out of my hands?"

The king was insulted that they wouldn't worship his god along with their own. When you have many gods, it is no big deal to add another. He didn't understand only worshipping one God. Wouldn't have approved if he had.

16 Shadrach, Meshach, and Abednego, answered and said to the king, "O Nebuchadnezzar, we are not careful to answer thee in this matter.

"We don't even have to think about our answer."

17 "If it be so, our God whom we serve is able to deliver us from the burning fiery furnace, and He will deliver us out of thine hand, O king.

18 "But if not, be it known unto thee, O king, that we will not serve thy gods, nor worship the golden image which thou hast set up."

"Our fate is not in your hands, oh king. Our God will decide if we live or die, not you. We won't deny Him or insult Him by worshiping your idol."

19 Then was Nebuchadnezzar full of fury, and the form of his visage was changed against Shadrach, Meshach, and Abednego: therefore he spake, and commanded that they should heat the furnace one seven times more than it was wont to be heated.

This furnace was probably either the heater for the palace or, more likely, the city bread oven. Either way, Nebuchadnezzar ordered it to be heated seven times hotter than it usually was.

20 And he commanded the most mighty men that were in his army to bind Shadrach, Meshach, and Abednego, and to cast them into the burning fiery furnace.

21 Then these men were bound in their coats, their hosen, and their hats, and their other garments, and were cast into the midst of the burning fiery furnace

22 Therefore because the king's commandment was urgent, and the furnace exceeding hot, the flame of the fire slew those men that took up Shadrach, Meshach, and Abednego.

The furnace was so hot that the men who threw the men into the fire died.

23 And these three men, Shadrach, Meshach, and Abednego, fell down bound into the midst of the burning fiery furnace.

24 Then Nebuchadnezzar the king was astonished, and rose up in haste, and spake, and said unto his counselors, "Did not we cast three men bound into the midst of the fire?" They answered and said unto the king, "True, O king."

25 He answered and said, "Lo, I see four men loose, walking in the midst of the fire, and they have no hurt; and the form of the fourth is like the Son of God."

The king was a bit shook up. He knew he threw three men in but saw four. And they weren't writhing around in agony. They were up and walking around. The fourth one looked like the son of a God (remember, the king is a polytheist at this point. He has no knowledge of the True God. The capital letters were added to the King James Bible in the 1700's)

26 Then Nebuchadnezzar came near to the mouth of the burning fiery furnace, and spake, and said, "Shadrach, Meshach, and Abednego, ye servants of the most high God, come forth, and come hither." Then Shadrach, Meshach, and Abednego, came forth of the midst of the fire.

27 And the Princes, governors, and captains, and the king's counselors, being gathered together, saw these men, upon whose bodies the fire had no power, nor was a hair of their head singed, neither were their coats changed, nor the smell of fire had passed on them.

They didn't even smell like smoke, much less have anything actually burnt. Remember, this is the same fire that killed the men that threw them into it.

28 Then Nebuchadnezzar spake, and said, "Blessed be the God of Shadrach, Meshach, and Abednego, who hath sent His angel, and delivered His servants that trusted in Him, and have changed the king's word, and yielded their bodies, that they might not serve nor worship any god, except their own God.

29 "Therefore I make a decree, that every people, nation, and language, which speak any thing amiss against the god of Shadrach, Meshach, and Abednego, shall be cut in pieces, and their houses shall be made a dunghill: because there is no other god that can deliver after this sort."

What, are we giving up on the fiery furnace as a punishment? Nebuchadnezzar decreed that everyone respect Shadrach, Meshach, and Abednego's God. I suspect he had a bit of fear of this new God.

30 Then the king promoted Shadrach, Meshach, and Abednego, in the province of Babylon.

Chapter 4
GOD TEACHES NEBUCHADNEZZAR A LESSON

Chapter four is a letter written by Nebuchadnezzar to his entire kingdom.

1 Nebuchadnezzar the king, unto all people, nations, and languages, that dwell in all the earth; Peace be multiplied unto you.

2 I thought it good to show the signs and wonders that the high God hath wrought toward me.

"I thought you should know what God has done to me."

3 How great are His signs! And how mighty are His wonders! His kingdom is an everlasting kingdom, and his dominion is from generation to generation.

"This God I am going to tell you about is the greatest God you have ever heard of."

4 I Nebuchadnezzar was at rest in mine house, and flourishing in my palace:

5 I saw a dream which made me afraid, and the thoughts upon my bed and the visions of my head troubled me.

6 Therefore made I a decree to bring in all the wise men of Babylon before me, that they might make known unto me the interpretation of the dream.

Sounds familiar. Nebuchadnezzar again has a dream, but this one doesn't just bother him; it scares him. He calls for interpreters.

7 Then came in the magicians, the astrologers, the Chaldeans, and the soothsayers: and I told the dream before them; but they did not make known unto me the interpretation thereof.

8 But at the last Daniel came in before me, whose name was Belteshazzar, according to the name of my god, and in whom is the spirit of the holy gods: and before him I told the dream, saying,

9 "O Belteshazzar, master of the magicians, because I know that the spirit of the holy gods is in thee, and no secret troubleth thee, tell me the visions of my dream that I have seen, and the interpretation thereof.

10 "Thus were the visions of mine head in my bed; I saw, and behold a tree in the midst of the earth, and the height thereof was great.

11 "The tree grew, and was strong, and the height thereof reached unto heaven, and the sight thereof to the end of all the earth:

The king sees a giant tree that fills the whole country.

12 "The leaves thereof were fair, and the fruit thereof much, and in it was meat for all: the beasts of the field had shadow under it, and the fowls of the heaven dwelt in the boughs thereof, and all flesh was fed of it.

This tree fed and housed all the birds and beasts and was very pretty.

13 "I saw in the visions of my head upon my bed, and, behold, a watcher and an holy one came down from heaven;

An angel? Or God Himself? Doesn't much matter as the message and outcome is the same.

14 "He cried aloud, and said thus, 'Hew down the tree, and cut off his branches, shake off his

leaves, and scatter his fruit: let the beasts get away from under it, and the fowls from his branches:

15 "'Nevertheless leave the stump of his roots in the earth, even with a band of iron and brass, in the tender grass of the field; and let it be wet with the dew of heaven, and let his portion be with the beasts in the grass of the earth:

The Holy One who came down from heaven commanded that the beautiful tree be cut down, but that its stump is preserved.

16 "'Let his heart be changed from man's, and let a beast's heart be given unto him; and let seven times pass over him.

The tree, who has a heart of a man, is to be given a heart of an animal for seven "times." We don't know how long "times" was. It had to be longer than days to have the effect on his hair and nails that it did. It was possibly weeks, months or seasons. Maybe even years, though I would think the kingdom would have suffered too much with its king gone for seven whole years.

17 "'This matter is by the decree of the watchers, and the demand by the word of the holy ones: to the intent that the living may know that the most High ruleth in the kingdom of men, and giveth it to whomsoever He will, and setteth up over it the basest of men.'

This will be done to show who the Boss is.

Watcher simply means angels, or messengers.

18 "This dream I king Nebuchadnezzar have seen. Now thou, O Belteshazzar, declare the interpretation thereof, forasmuch as all the wise men of my kingdom are not able to make known unto me the interpretation: but thou art able; for the spirit of the holy gods is in thee."

Nebuchadnezzar had faith that Daniel would be able to tell him what his dream meant.

19 Then Daniel, whose name was Belteshazzar, was astonied for one hour, and his thoughts troubled him. The king spake, and said, "Belteshazzar, let not the dream, or the interpretation thereof, trouble thee..."

Daniel is so shook up by the meaning of the dream he can't speak for an hour. The king finally tells him to not be afraid but just speak up.

...Belteshazzar answered and said, "My lord, the dream be to them that hate thee, and the interpretation thereof to thine enemies.

Daniel says "This dream is for the information of those who are your enemies."

20 "The tree that thou sawest, which grew, and was strong, whose height reached unto the heaven, and the sight thereof to all the earth;

21 "Whose leaves were fair, and the fruit thereof much, and in it was meat for all; under which the beasts of the field dwelt, and upon whose branches the fowls of the heaven had their habitation:

22 "It is thou, O king, that art grown and become strong: for thy greatness is grown, and reacheth unto heaven, and thy dominion to the end of the earth.

The tree is Nebuchadnezzar. He is a very great man whose influence is felt all over the known world and who has provided a golden age for the region.

23 "And whereas the king saw a watcher and an holy one coming down from heaven, and saying,

'Hew the tree down, and destroy it; yet leave the stump of the roots thereof in the earth, even with a band of iron and brass, in the tender grass of the field; and let it be wet with the dew of heaven, and let his portion be with the beasts of the field, till seven times pass over him;'

A band of metal around a tree stump keeps it from disintegrating.

24 "This is the interpretation, O king, and this is the decree of the most High, which is come upon my lord the king:

25 "That they shall drive thee from men, and thy dwelling shall be with the beasts of the field, and they shall make thee to eat grass as oxen, and they shall wet thee with the dew of heaven, and seven times shall pass over thee, till thou know that the most High ruleth in the kingdom of men, and giveth it to whomsoever he will.

Nebuchadnezzar is going to be insane for a time. He will think himself an animal eating grass and not doing any grooming. This will last until he acknowledges the One True God.

26 "And whereas they commanded to leave the stump of the tree roots; thy kingdom shall be sure unto thee, after that thou shalt have known that the heavens do rule.

"As soon as you realize God is God, He will give you back your health and your kingdom."

27 "Wherefore, O king, let my counsel be acceptable unto thee, and break off thy sins by righteousness, and thine iniquities by showing mercy

*to the poor; if it may be a lengthening of thy
tranquility."*

Daniel advises the king to change his ways now and
not wait for God's lesson to come on him.

28 All this came upon the king Nebuchadnezzar.

*29 At the end of twelve months he walked in the
palace of the kingdom of Babylon.*

*30 The king spake, and said, "Is not this great
Babylon, that I have built for the house of the
kingdom by the might of my power, and for the honor
of my majesty?"*

A year later the king is walking around his palace
(possibly the Hanging Gardens of Babylon) and boasts
about how strong and great he is.

*31 While the word was in the king's mouth, there
fell a voice from heaven, saying, "O king
Nebuchadnezzar, to thee it is spoken; The kingdom is
departed from thee.*

*32 "And they shall drive thee from men, and thy
dwelling shall be with the beasts of the field: they
shall make thee to eat grass as oxen, and seven times
shall pass over thee, until thou know that the most
High ruleth in the kingdom of men, and giveth it to
whomsoever He will."*

The king hears a voice repeating Daniel's
interpretation of the dream.

*33 The same hour was the thing fulfilled upon
Nebuchadnezzar: and he was driven from men, and
did eat grass as oxen, and his body was wet with the
dew of heaven, till his hairs were grown like eagles'
feathers, and his nails like birds' claws.*

At that instant Nebuchadnezzar became insane and believed he was an animal. They chased him out of the palace. He lived as a wild animal.

34 And at the end of the days I Nebuchadnezzar lifted up mine eyes unto heaven, and mine understanding returned unto me, and I blessed the most High, and I praised and honored Him that liveth forever, whose dominion is an everlasting dominion, and His kingdom is from generation to generation:

35 And all the inhabitants of the earth are reputed as nothing: and He doeth according to His will in the army of heaven, and among the inhabitants of the earth: and none can stay His hand, or say unto Him, "What doest thou?"

He finally acknowledges God and His greatness.

36 At the same time my reason returned unto me; and for the glory of my kingdom, mine honor and brightness returned unto me; and my counselors and my lords sought unto me; and I was established in my kingdom, and excellent majesty was added unto me.

God kept His promise and as soon as Nebuchadnezzar accepted Him as the True God, his entire kingdom was restored.

37 Now I Nebuchadnezzar praise and extol and honor the King of heaven, all whose works are truth, and His ways judgment: and those that walk in pride He is able to abase.

It is possible that Nebuchadnezzar was saved from this point on. He just might be in heaven with us.

33

Chapter 5
THE HANDWRITING ON THE WALL

Belshazzar was probably Nebuchadnezzar's grandson or grandson-in-law. There seems to have been quite a mix up as to who got the throne after Nebuchadnezzar died. We know that Belshazzar's father did not like to rule, but preferred to play archeologist. He was off digging in the dirt, leaving Belshazzar in charge.

1 Belshazzar the king made a great feast to a thousand of his lords, and drank wine before the thousand.

2 Belshazzar, while he tasted the wine, commanded to bring the golden and silver vessels which his father Nebuchadnezzar had taken out of the temple which was in Jerusalem; that the king, and his princes, his wives, and his concubines, might drink therein.

The Bible uses the term "father" to refer to either the direct male parent or grandparent, or occasionally any male ancestor.

3 Then they brought the golden vessels that were taken out of the temple of the house of God which was at Jerusalem; and the king, and his princes, his wives, and his concubines, drank in them.

4 They drank wine, and praised the gods of gold, and of silver, of brass, of iron, of wood, and of stone.

It sounds like they just decided to have a party here. The truth is that the city is under siege at this moment. This party was probably intended to be a morale booster or to show defiance to the enemy.

34

Babylon was surrounded by a huge wall with two gates in it to allow part of the Euphrates River to flow through the middle of town. Heavy iron gates were lowered into the river every night to keep enemy boats from sailing into town and conquering them (they were opened during the day so merchants could sail their wares into the city easily). Because of their water supply, a siege would actually be very unsuccessful. Yet the Medo-Persian army is outside the gates of the city at this moment, hoping to find a way in to conquer their overlords.

5 In the same hour came forth fingers of a man's hand, and wrote over against the candlestick upon the plaster of the wall of the king's palace: and the king saw the part of the hand that wrote.

A disembodied hand floating in the air, writing on the wall.

6 Then the king's countenance was changed, and his thoughts troubled him, so that the joints of his loins were loosed, and his knees smote one against another.

He was scared.

7 The king cried aloud to bring in the astrologers, the Chaldeans, and the soothsayers. And the king spake, and said to the wise men of Babylon, "Whosoever shall read this writing, and show me the interpretation thereof, shall be clothed with scarlet, and have a chain of gold about his neck, and shall be the third ruler in the kingdom."

Since his father was technically the first ruler and Belshazzar the second, the highest rank available to promote anyone to was third ruler.

8 Then came in all the king's wise men: but they could not read the writing, nor make known to the king the interpretation thereof.

9 Then was king Belshazzar greatly troubled, and his countenance was changed in him, and his lords were astonied.

10 Now the queen by reason of the words of the king and his lords came into the banquet house: and the queen spake and said, "O king, live forever: let not thy thoughts trouble thee, nor let thy countenance be changed:

This was probably the king's mother or grandmother; a woman who had seen Daniel in action in her youth.

11 "There is a man in thy kingdom, in whom is the spirit of the holy gods; and in the days of thy father light and understanding and wisdom, like the wisdom of the gods, was found in him; whom the king Nebuchadnezzar thy father, the king, I say, thy father, made master of the magicians, astrologers, Chaldeans, and soothsayers;

12 "Forasmuch as an excellent spirit, and knowledge, and understanding, interpreting of dreams, and showing of hard sentences, and dissolving of doubts, were found in the same Daniel, whom the king named Belteshazzar: now let Daniel be called, and he will show the interpretation."

13 Then was Daniel brought in before the king. And the king spake and said unto Daniel, "Art thou that Daniel, which art of the children of the captivity of Judah, whom the king my father brought out of Jewry?

14 "I have even heard of thee, that the spirit of the gods is in thee, and that light and understanding and excellent wisdom is found in thee.

15 "And now the wise men, the astrologers, have been brought in before me, that they should read this writing, and make known unto me the interpretation thereof: but they could not show the interpretation of the thing:

16 "And I have heard of thee, that thou canst make interpretations, and dissolve doubts: now if thou canst read the writing, and make known to me the interpretation thereof, thou shalt be clothed with scarlet, and have a chain of gold about thy neck, and shalt be the third ruler in the kingdom."

17 Then Daniel answered and said before the king, "Let thy gifts be to thyself, and give thy rewards to another; yet I will read the writing unto the king, and make known to him the interpretation.

Daniel was not interested in material rewards.

We get the idea he didn't really like Belshazzar, though it sounded earlier like he was quite fond of Nebuchadnezzar.

18 "O thou king, the most high God gave Nebuchadnezzar thy father a kingdom, and majesty, and glory, and honor:

"Everything your ancestor had came from God."

19 "And for the majesty that He gave him, all people, nations, and languages, trembled and feared before him: whom he would he slew; and whom he would he kept alive; and whom he would he set up; and whom he would he put down.

20 "But when his heart was lifted up, and his mind hardened in pride, he was deposed from his kingly throne, and they took his glory from him:

21 "And he was driven from the sons of men; and his heart was made like the beasts, and his dwelling was with the wild asses: they fed him with grass like oxen, and his body was wet with the dew of heaven; till he knew that the most high God ruled in the kingdom of men, and that he appointeth over it whomsoever he will.

Daniel reminds Belshazzar of Nebuchadnezzar's lesson from God in humility.

22 "And thou his son, O Belshazzar, hast not humbled thine heart, though thou knewest all this;

"Son" can mean any male descendant.

Belshazzar chose to ignore his own history. He chose to be prideful.

23 "But hast lifted up thyself against the Lord of heaven; and they have brought the vessels of his house before thee, and thou, and thy lords, thy wives, and thy concubines, have drunk wine in them; and thou hast praised the gods of silver, and gold, of brass, iron, wood, and stone, which see not, nor hear, nor know: and the God in whose hand thy breath is, and whose are all thy ways, hast thou not glorified:

24 "Then was the part of the hand sent from Him; and this writing was written.

25 "And this is the writing that was written, MENE, MENE, TEKEL, UPHARSIN.

26 "This is the interpretation of the thing: MENE; God hath numbered thy kingdom, and finished it.

"Mene" means "to number."

"Your kingdom has a limit of the number of days it will last, and that limit has been reached."

27 "TEKEL; Thou art weighed in the balances, and art found wanting.

"Tekel" means "to weigh."

"God has judged you and you have come up short."

28 "PERES; Thy kingdom is divided, and given to the Medes and Persians."

"Peres" means "to divide."

"You lose"

(The U in upharsin simply means "and")

29 Then commanded Belshazzar, and they clothed Daniel with scarlet, and put a chain of gold about his neck, and made a proclamation concerning him, that he should be the third ruler in the kingdom.

Belshazzar kept his word, even though Daniel gave him a negative interpretation.

30 In that night was Belshazzar the king of the Chaldeans slain.

The priests of the city were tired of Belshazzar's irreligious behavior. He evidently frequently insulted all the "gods," not just the True God. While Belshazzar was partying, the priests snuck out and opened the gates to the river.

Meanwhile, the Medo- Persian army had diverted the part of the river that ran under the wall. The whole army simply marched into the city and took it. This was prophesied in Isaiah 45:1:

"Thus saith the Lord to His anointed, to Cyrus, whose right hand I have holden, to subdue nations before him; and I will loose the loins of kings, to open before him the two leaved gates; and the gates shall not be shut;"

Isaiah prophesied around 675 BC. Babylon was conquered in 459 BC.

31 And Darius the Median took the kingdom, being about threescore and two years (62) old.

Cyrus the Great's mother and wife were both Median princess. We know from Greek histories that Cyrus's Uncle Father-in-Law was the king of Mede, and co-ruled with Cyrus over a combined empire; Medo-Persia. When he died (shortly after the conquest of Babylon) Cyrus inherited the Mede throne. Some evidence says Cyrus was elsewhere fighting a different war when Babylon fell and his uncle was the general who was actually in charge of the attack, though the evidence is not yet clear since it comes from a couple of different sources that don't agree. So it is likely "Darius the Mede" was King Darius of Mede, brother to Cyrus the Great's mom, and daddy to his wife.

Anyway, Babylon is now dead.

Chapter 6

Medo Persian Empire

DANIEL IN THE LION'S DEN

1 It pleased Darius (The Mede) **to set over the kingdom an hundred and twenty princes, which should be over the whole kingdom;**

Darius is setting up his government. He chooses to put 120 men in charge, answerable to three men who were answerable to him.

2 And over these three presidents; of whom Daniel was first: that the princes might give accounts unto them, and the king should have no damage.

3 Then this Daniel was preferred above the presidents and princes, because an excellent spirit was in him; and the king thought to set him over the whole realm.

The king liked Daniel so much he was going to make him vice-king.

4 Then the presidents and princes sought to find occasion against Daniel concerning the kingdom; but they could find none occasion nor fault; forasmuch as he was faithful, neither was there any error or fault found in him.

The other bureaucrats were jealous of Daniel and tried to find something to get him in trouble. But Daniel lived a righteous life and they couldn't find even one small thing to accuse him of wrong doing.

Could you stand such an examination?

5 Then said these men, "We shall not find any occasion against this Daniel, except we find it against him concerning the law of his God."

They knew the only way they were going to get Daniel was through his religion.

6 Then these presidents and princes assembled together to the king, and said thus unto him, "King Darius, live forever.

7 "All the presidents of the kingdom, the governors, and the princes, the counselors, and the captains, have consulted together to establish a royal statute, and to make a firm decree, that whosoever shall ask a petition of any god or man for thirty days,

save of thee, O king, he shall be cast into the den of lions.

They knew Daniel's prayer habits and knew his integrity. They knew they had him.

8 "Now, O king, establish the decree, and sign the writing, that it be not changed, according to the law of the Medes and Persians, which altereth not."

Once a law was signed by the king, it could never be changed. This was not true in most countries. Kings could arbitrarily change laws to suit themselves and exempt themselves from them. But in Medo-Persia even the king was bound by The Law.

This is where we get our country's "equal in the eyes of the law." Everyone from the president to the bum in the gutter is supposed to be subject to the same laws. This keeps the powers that be from passing unjust, cruel or frivolous laws.

9 Wherefore king Darius signed the writing and the decree.

His ego got the better of him and he doesn't seem to have noticed that Daniel was not with them.

10 Now when Daniel knew that the writing was signed, he went into his house; and his windows being open in his chamber toward Jerusalem, he kneeled upon his knees three times a day, and prayed, and gave thanks before his God, as he did aforetime.

Daniel had a powerful prayer life and he didn't let a little thing like the threat of death get in his way. He knew who really had control of his life.

11 Then these men assembled, and found Daniel praying and making supplication before his God.

12 Then they came near, and spake before the king concerning the king's decree; "Hast thou not signed a decree, that every man that shall ask a petition of any God or man within thirty days, save of thee, O king, shall be cast into the den of lions?" The king answered and said, "The thing is true, according to the law of the Medes and Persians, which altereth not."

13 Then answered they and said before the king, "That Daniel, which is of the children of the captivity of Judah, regardeth not thee, O king, nor the decree that thou hast signed, but maketh his petition three times a day."

14 Then the king, when he heard these words, was sore displeased with himself, and set his heart on Daniel to deliver him: and he labored till the going down of the sun to deliver him.

The king was so upset he spent the day trying to find a loophole. He really liked Daniel and knew he had been tricked.

15 Then these men assembled unto the king, and said unto the king, "Know, O king, that the law of the Medes and Persians is, that no decree nor statute which the king establisheth may be changed."

16 Then the king commanded, and they brought Daniel, and cast him into the den of lions. Now the king spake and said unto Daniel, "Thy God whom thou servest continually, he will deliver thee."

What a statement of faith! And from an unbeliever at that!

17 And a stone was brought, and laid upon the mouth of the den; and the king sealed it with his own

signet, and with the signet of his lords; that the purpose might not be changed concerning Daniel.

They covered the edge of the stone with wax and put their signet rings in it to leave an impression. If anyone had come along and opened the den, the impressions would have been broken. The fact that the princes sealed it too meant the king couldn't even sneak Daniel out in the night.

18 Then the king went to his palace, and passed the night fasting: neither were instruments of music brought before him: and his sleep went from him.

The king spent the whole night worrying.

19 Then the king arose very early in the morning, and went in haste unto the den of lions.

20 And when he came to the den, he cried with a lamentable voice unto Daniel: and the king spake and said to Daniel, "O Daniel, servant of the living God, is thy God, whom thou servest continually, able to deliver thee from the lions?"

He recognized that if there was salvation for Daniel, it came from his God.

21 Then said Daniel unto the king, "O king, live forever.

22 "My God hath sent his angel, and hath shut the lions' mouths, that they have not hurt me: forasmuch as before him innocency was found in me; and also before thee, O king, have I done no hurt."

God knew that Daniel was innocent and prevented him from being damaged. Do you suppose he used a lion as a pillow that night?

23 Then was the king exceedingly glad for him, and commanded that they should take Daniel up out of the den. So Daniel was taken up out of the den, and no manner of hurt was found upon him, because he believed in his God.

Not even a scratch!

24 And the king commanded, and they brought those men which had accused Daniel, and they cast them into the den of lions, them, their children, and their wives; and the lions had the mastery of them, and brake all their bones in pieces or ever they came at the bottom of the den.

The king was mad enough he had the men who had fooled him and their wives and children thrown into the den. Turns out angels really had protected Daniel. Those lions were so hungry they broke every bone before the people even hit the ground. They hadn't left Daniel alone because of just being too full to be interested.

25 Then king Darius wrote unto all people, nations, and languages, that dwell in all the earth; "Peace be multiplied unto you.

26 "I make a decree, that in every dominion of my kingdom men tremble and fear before the God of Daniel: for He is the living God, and stedfast forever, and His kingdom that which shall not be destroyed, and His dominion shall be even unto the end.

27 "He delivereth and rescueth, and He worketh signs and wonders in heaven and in earth, who hath delivered Daniel from the power of the lions."

He did not outlaw the worship of others gods, but did command that everyone, at minimum, have a great fear of the True God.

Jewish history tells us that Darius and Cyrus both worked towards changing their countries' religion from

polytheistic Baal and Ashera worship to Zoroaster, which at this time in history was a monotheistic religion, probably a corruption of Judaism. Maybe this incident was what started them on this path.

28 So this Daniel prospered in the reign of Darius, and in the reign of Cyrus the Persian.

This ends the historical part of the book of Daniel. The rest of the book is a record of his visions. They begin in the reign of Belshazzar and go through the reign of Cyrus.

Chapter 7
FOUR GREAT BEASTS

1 In the first year of Belshazzar king of Babylon, Daniel had a dream, and visions of his head upon his bed. Then he wrote the dream and told the sum of the matters.

This is somewhere around 462$_{BC}$.

I have rearranged the verses so that we only read the vision once, side-by-side with the interpretation.

15 I Daniel was grieved in my spirit in the midst of my body, and the visions of my head troubled me.

16 I came near unto one of them that stood by, and asked him the truth of all this. So he told me, and made me know the interpretation of the things.

This was an angel he saw in his vision.

2 Daniel spake and said: "I saw in my vision by night and behold the four winds of heaven strove upon the great sea.

3 And four great beasts came up from the sea, diverse one from another.

17 (The Angel speaks) These great beasts, which are four, are four kings, which shall arise out of the earth.

This is the interpretation the angel gave him.

4 (Daniel:) The first was like a lion, and it had eagle's wings: I beheld till the wings thereof were plucked, and it was lifted up from the earth, and made stand upon the feet as a man, and a man's heart was given to it.

Nebuchadnezzar after his time as a beast of the field. The "man's heart" signified his acceptance of God.

5 And behold another beast, a second, like to a bear, and it raised up itself on one side, and it had three ribs in the mouth of it between the teeth of it: and they said thus unto it, 'Arise, devour much flesh.'

Persia, under Cyrus the Great, destroyed Lydia, Babylon, and Egypt. All three completely ended as world powers at this point. These are the three ribs.

6 After this I beheld, and lo another, like a leopard, which had upon the back of it four wings of a fowl; the beast had also four heads; and dominion was given to it.

Alexander the Great and his kingdom, which was divided after his death. This division took seven years of war between his four generals. Ptolemy (or Ptolemeaus) Lagi became the Egyptian king and gave part of his kingdom to his favorite under-general, Seleucus, who defeated one of the other general/kings and took Syria as well as part of Egypt. There is little or no disagreement about the interpretation up to this point.

7 After this I saw in the night visions, and behold a fourth beast, dreadful and terrible, and strong exceedingly; and it had great iron teeth: it devoured and brake in pieces, and stamped the residue with the feet of it: and it was diverse from all the beasts that were before it; and it had ten horns

19 Then I would know the truth of the fourth beast, which was diverse from all the others, exceeding dreadful, whose teeth were of iron, and his nails of brass; which devoured, brake in pieces, and stamped the residue with his feet;

23 (Angel) Thus he said, 'The fourth beast shall be the fourth kingdom upon earth, which shall be

diverse from all kingdoms, and shall devour the whole earth (land)**, and shall tread it down, and break it in pieces.**

This fourth beast is the kingdom of Syria; specifically the family of the Seleucids. Josephus and the Maccabees tell us the Seleucids were very cruel to the Jews. Their armies (the iron teeth) horribly mistreated the people (using mostly iron weapons).

The Syrian empire covered at least as much territory as Rome (though fewer people), including the whole area of the Babylonian Empire, the country Daniel was writing this from; "whole earth" means "whole kingdom," in the original language. In Daniel's case at this time in history, that would mean the Babylonian Empire.

20 (Daniel) **And of the ten horns that were in his head,...**

24 (Angel) **And the ten horns out of this kingdom are ten kings that shall arise:...**

Ptolemy Lagi gave Syria to his general...

1) 312-281$_{BC}$ Seleucus I Nicator

2) Ptolemy Soter of Egypt controlled Israel for a short time.

3) 281-261$_{BC}$ Antiochus I Soter

4) 261-246$_{BC}$ Antiochus II Theos

5) 246-225$_{BC}$ Seleucus II Callinicos

6) 225-223$_{BC}$ Seleucus III Ceraunos

7) 223-187$_{BC}$ Antiochus III The Great

8) 187-175$_{BC}$ Seleucus IV Philopater (son of Antiochus III, brother to Antiochus IV)

9) Heliodorus (the tax collecter)

The son of Seleucus IV, never ruled but should have.

10) 175-164$_{BC}$ Antiochus IV Epiphanies

This was the Syrian empire in full force. They totally destroyed everyone they conquered. Rome and Greece didn't usually destroy total countries. They usually just subdued them and then left them alone as long as they paid their taxes and didn't cause too much trouble. This wasn't true of Syria. They were down-right mean.

8 *(Daniel)* ***I considered the horns, and, behold, there came up among them another little horn*** (Antiochus IV), ***before whom there were three of the first horns plucked up by the roots*** (he was directly involved in the downfall of three other kings; his brother, the tax collector, and his nephew who should have reigned): ***and, behold, in this horn were eyes like the eyes of man, and a mouth speaking great things.***

(Angel) **... and of the other which came up, and before whom three fell; even of that horn that had eyes, and a mouth that spake very great things, whose look was more stout than his fellows.**

21 *(Daniel)* ***I beheld, and the same horn made war with the saints, and prevailed against them;***

The little horn is Antiochus Epiphanies, the last of the ten kings. He got the throne by having his nephew taken captive in Rome and having a buddy depose the murderer of his brother (who he had backed). He was a man of great ingenuity, and therefore is said to have eyes like the eyes of a man; and he was very bold and daring, had a mouth speaking great things.

Antiochus IV was the only king in the history of Israel who demanded they leave their God, not just incorporate his own. In fact, he commanded his entire kingdom, including his own country, to worship Jupiter instead of their native gods.

Antiochus IV used deceit, flattery, and bribes to get and establish his kingdom.

22 Until the Ancient of Days came, and judgment was given to the saints of the most High; and the time came that the saints (True lovers of God) **possessed the kingdom** (of God).

The Ancient of Days is God pronouncing judgment on Antiochus (He killed him). After this, the Jews ruled themselves (more or less, off and on, until Rome conquered them; about a hundred years.)

24 (Angel) **... and another shall rise after them** (Antiochus IV Epiphanies)**; and he shall be diverse from the first, and he shall subdue three kings.**

Brother, nephew, general/tax collector.

25 And he (the horn) **shall speak great words against the most High, and shall wear out the saints of the most High, and think to change times and laws: and they** (the Jews) **shall be given into his** (the horn's) **hand until a time and times and the dividing of time.**

Antiochus was especially mean to Israel for about three and a half years. He thought he was a god and changed the calendar.

26 But the judgment shall sit, and they (the Jews) **shall take away his dominion, to consume and to destroy it unto the end** (of Antiochus' kingdom).

The Maccabees kicked him out.

Some assign this beast to Rome and this horn to Nero, but that is problematic. Nero was the sixth or seventh (depending on if you count the general who ruled for Tiberius for a short time) ruler of the Roman Empire.

The tenth emperor was Vespasian who was the emperor from AD 69- 79, but he was not a proud boaster, nor did he in anyway fit the description of the little horn. (His son, Titus, became emperor after him in 79). If you do count the ruling general, the tenth emperor was Vitelius who ruled a whole year and did nothing remarkable except fight for the throne with Otho for half that time. In fact, if you don't count Otho or the general, the tenth emperor was Titus who was a relatively meek (though quite unlucky) emperor (there were earthquakes and volcanoes and The Plague during his two year reign).

Augustus, the second Emperor of Rome, was the one who changed the calendar. However, the character of the little horn describes Antiochus IV perfectly.

9 (Daniel) I beheld till the thrones were cast down, and the Ancient of days did sit, whose garment was white as snow, and the hair of His head like the pure wool: His throne was like the fiery flame, and His wheels as burning fire.

God on the throne.

10 A fiery stream issued and came forth from before Him: thousand thousands ministered unto Him, and ten thousand times ten thousand stood before Him: the judgment was set, and the books were opened.

13 I saw in the night visions, and, behold, one like the Son of man came with the clouds of heaven, and came to the Ancient of days, and they brought him (Christ) *near before Him.* (God)

14 And there was given Him (Christ) *dominion, and glory, and a kingdom, that all people, nations, and languages, should serve Him: His dominion is an everlasting dominion, which shall not pass away, and His kingdom that which shall not be destroyed.*

The kingdom of heaven, which began at Calvary. This kingdom has never been and never will be destroyed. It has citizens in every country of the world. Its King rules the nations now, putting those in charge that He wants in charge and removing them when He chooses.

18 (Angel) **But the saints of the Most High will receive the kingdom and will possess it forever- yes forever and ever.**

27 And the kingdom and dominion, and the greatness of the kingdom under the whole heaven, shall be given to the people of the saints of the most High, whose kingdom is an everlasting kingdom, and all dominions shall serve and obey him.

Daniel is shown up to the time of Christ and His victory- the institution of the Kingdom of God at Calvary.

His attention, however, goes back to the little horn.

11 (Daniel) I beheld then because of the voice of the great words which the horn spake: (back to Antiochus IV) *I beheld even till the beast* (the last of the four beasts in Daniel's vision) *was slain, and his body destroyed, and given to the burning flame.*

The Roman army under Pompey destroyed the Syrian Empire in 63 BC.

12 As concerning the rest of the beasts, they had their dominion taken away: yet their lives were prolonged for a season and time.

These nations still exist, more or less, in a VERY reduced state; Iraq [Babylon], Iran [Persia], and Greece

28 Hitherto is the end of the matter. As for me Daniel, my cogitations much troubled me, and my countenance changed in me: but I kept the matter in my heart.

This is the end of this dream. It upset Daniel, but he didn't talk to anyone about it.

Chapter 8
THE RAM AND THE GOAT

1 In the third year of the reign of king Belshazzar a vision appeared unto me, even unto me Daniel, after that which appeared unto me at the first.

This dream occurred two years after the previous dream.

2 In my vision I saw myself in the citadel of Susa in the province of Elam; in the vision I was beside the Ulai Canal.

Susa became one of the capital cities of the Persian Empire. The Ulai may have been the eastern branch of the Choasper.

15 And it came to pass, when I, even I Daniel, had seen the vision, and sought for the meaning, then, behold, there stood before me as the appearance of a man

16 And I heard a man's voice between the banks of Ulai, which called, and said, 'Gabriel, make this man to understand the vision.'

17 So he came near where I stood: and when he came, I was afraid, and fell upon my face: but he said unto me, 'Understand, O son of man: for at the time of the end (of Israel) **shall be the vision.'**

Gabriel tells Daniel that this vision is about the rest of the history of Israel. At this point in history, Israel/Judah (the book of Daniel uses the terms interchangeably, just meaning "descendants of Jacob") is in captivity to Babylon. It is possible Daniel is afraid its history is already over. God shows him what is really left.

18 Now as he was speaking with me, I was in a deep sleep on my face toward the ground: but he touched me, and set me upright.

19 And he said, 'Behold, I will make thee know what shall be in the last end of the indignation (the last beast seen in the last dream)**: for at the time appointed the end** (of the indignation) **shall be.'**

3 Then I lifted up mine eyes, and saw, and, behold, there stood before the river a ram which had two horns: and the two horns were high; but one was higher than the other, and the higher came up last.

20 The ram which thou sawest having two horns are the kings of Media and Persia.

Persia was the newer kingdom, but became bigger than Media. At the time of this vision, they were both gaining power.

4 I saw the ram pushing westward, and northward, and southward; so that no beasts might stand before him, neither was there any that could deliver out of his hand; but he did according to his will, and became great.

It was very shortly after this dream that Medo-Persia conquered Babylon. This made them bigger than the Babylonian Empire.

5 And as I was considering, behold, an he goat came from the west on the face of the whole earth, and touched not the ground: and the goat had a notable horn between his eyes.

21 And the rough goat is the king of Grecia: and the great horn that is between his eyes is the first king.

Alexander the Great

6 And he came to the ram that had two horns, which I had seen standing before the river, and ran unto him in the fury of his power.

Darius the Persian had defeated Alexander's dad Phillip, who had died in battle with the Persians. Alexander went after Persia partly in revenge. There had been wars between the two countries for years. Alexander hunted Darius down and would have killed him if a scared general from Persia hadn't done it just before.

7 And I saw him come close unto the ram, and he was moved with choler against him, and smote the ram, and brake his two horns: and there was no power in the ram to stand before him, but he cast him down to the ground, and stamped upon him: and there was none that could deliver the ram out of his hand.

Alexander flat destroyed all remnants of power from the Persian and Babylonian Empires.

8 Therefore the he goat waxed very great: and when he was strong, the great horn was broken; and for it came up four notable ones toward the four winds of heaven.

22 Now that being broken, whereas four stood up for it, four kingdoms shall stand up out of the nation, but not in his power.

Alexander reached the Indus River in India. He wanted to go further, but his soldiers rebelled and threatened to leave him if he did. He returned to Babylonia where he died (poisoning or maybe malaria. We don't know.) He was thirty-two.

His four major Generals fought over the kingdom, killing his son, wives, mother and any other relatives they

could find. After seven years of civil war, the kingdom was divided into four parts:

Antigonus won Greece (Mediterranean to central Greece, Near Asia)

Ptolemy Lagi won Egypt and southern Syria. Ptolemy gave Syria to his favorite general, Seleucid who captured Antigonus' Asian territory.

Cassander won Macedonia (northern modern Greece)

Lysimachus won Thrace (by the Black sea)

9 And out of one of them (Egypt) **came forth a little horn** (Seleucus)**, which waxed exceeding great, toward the south, and toward the east, and toward the pleasant land** (Israel).

10 And it waxed great, even to the host of heaven; and it cast down some of the host and of the stars to the ground, and stamped upon them.

Antiochus IV of the Seleucid family killed many Israelites, especially the priests. God's people are often represented as stars in the Bible. In this case the "host of heaven" is talking about the Israelites who truly loved God.

11 Yea, he magnified himself even to the prince of the host, and by him the daily sacrifice was taken away, and the place of his sanctuary was cast down.

Antiochus IV stopped the daily sacrifice for a time. He considered himself a god, and magnified himself to the same level as Jesus, the Prince of the host (or kingdom of God).

12 And an host was given him (the little horn) *against the daily sacrifice by reason of transgression,*

*and it cast down the truth to the ground; and it
practiced, and prospered.*

Because of the rebellion of the Jews and to prove
God's power, this was allowed.

**23 " And in the latter time of their kingdom,
when the transgressors are come to the full, a king of
fierce countenance, and understanding dark
sentences, shall stand up.**

24 And his (Antiochus IV) **power shall be mighty,
but not by his own power** (by God's allowance with
some help from Rome): **and he shall destroy
wonderfully, and shall prosper, and practice, and
shall destroy the mighty and the holy people.**

**25 And through his policy also he shall cause
craft to prosper in his hand; and he shall magnify
himself in his heart, and by peace shall destroy many:
he shall also stand up against the Prince of princes;
but he shall be broken without hand.**

Antiochus III (of the Seleucid dynasty) was
succeeded by his son Seleucid IV Philopator (187- 175
BC). In order to collect taxes, Seleucid IV sent his tax
collector to rob the Jerusalem temple. However,
Heliodorus (the tax collector) had Seleucid IV killed and
assumed the throne.

Seleucid IV's brother had been captured by the
Romans in a war with their father. Seleucid IV sent his
son, Demetrius, to Rome as a hostage trade for his
brother Antiochus IV just before his death. Antiochus IV
secretly negotiated with Rome for the Seleucid throne.
Rome agreed to keep his nephew, Demetrius, as a
hostage in exchange for extra taxes.

Antiochus IV had secretly supported Heliodorus in his assassination of Seleucid IV. Now, the king of Pergamus was given a portion of the Syrian kingdom by the Romans for assisting them in the wars against the Seleucids. This king kicked Heliodorus (the tax collector) out (with Antiochus IV's help) and put Antiochus IV on the throne.

So, Antiochus IV Epiphanes took control of the kingdom of Syria and reigned from 175 BC to 164 BC. He stole from the treasury and Jewish temples, roamed around in Roman officer clothes, and drank and caroused with the lowest of the people. He was way more wicked than previous rulers. He orchestrated the death of the Jewish High-Priest and scores of priests and scribes (They refused to eat pork so he killed them) and sold the High-Priest position to the highest bidders. He took control of the Jerusalem temple, ended the daily sacrifices, sacrificed unclean animals on the temple altar and altars throughout Judea, performed or allowed acts of sexual perversion within the temple, placed an idol in the temple, collected the sacred Hebrew scrolls, threw them to the ground, and burned them in order to eliminate the Holy Laws from the land. He also plundered the temple treasury.

2 Maccabees 9 tells us that God struck Antiochus IV down with an incurable pain in his bowels. Antiochus IV was riding in a chariot when he fell out and his body was racked throughout. Living for a brief time, he became so infected that flesh fell off his bones and produced a horrid stench. He died without dignity- destroyed, but not by human hands.

13 Then I heard one saint speaking, and another saint said unto that certain saint which spake, "How long shall be the vision concerning the daily sacrifice, and the transgression of desolation, to give both the sanctuary and the host to be trodden under foot?"

14 And he said unto me, "Unto two thousand and three hundred days; then shall the sanctuary be cleansed."

Antiochus IV desecrated the Temple alter on Chislev 15, 168 BC. The Jews celebrated its reconsecration on Chislev 25, 165 BC, 1150 days or 2300 "daily" sacrifices later (one in the evening and one in the morning.) [As recorded in the books of the Maccabees]

26 " And the vision of the evening and the morning which was told is true: wherefore shut thou up the vision; for it shall be for many days.

It would be about 250 years before these prophecies would be useful to anyone.

27 And I Daniel fainted, and was sick certain days; afterward I rose up, and did the king's business; and I was astonished at the vision, but none understood it.

Chapter 9
SEVENTY YEARS AND SEVENTY WEEKS

1 In the first year of Darius son of Ahasuerus, of the seed of the Medes, which was made king over the realm of the Chaldeans;

This Darius the Persian was the son-in-law of Ahasuerus and Esther. He came to power, according to Jewish histories, after executing King Hamedetha.

Ahasuerus, son of Darius of Mede, had not liked the arrangement of Cyrus inheriting the kingdom after his father's death. He "took care of" Cyrus. This victory was probably what they were celebrating in the beginning of the book of Esther where Vashti was deposed.

Ahasuerus was (according to Jewish history) assassinated by one of his ministers, who ruled just a month before Hamedetha took over. Ahasuerus had continued to move the country towards the Zoroaster religion, but Hamedetha moved it back to Baal worship and polytheism.

Darius, son of a Persian nobleman, married the princess, removed Hamedetha, and took the country back to Zoroaster.

In this case "son" means "son-in-law and heir."

2 In the first year of his reign, I, Daniel understood by books the number of the years, whereof the word of the LORD came to Jeremiah the prophet, that he would accomplish seventy years in the desolations of Jerusalem.

Jeremiah (who was a priest) was about 34 when Daniel was carried off captive. Somehow, Daniel had Jeremiah's prophecies with him in Babylon. There is a Jeremiah listed in the book of Nehemiah as one of the

63

priests that returned to Babylon, but we have no way of knowing if it is the same Jeremiah. If it was, he was a very old man, though God did promise him he would go back to Canaan personally after the captivity, so it's entirely possible Nehemiah's Jerimiah is the author of the book by the same name.

3 And I set my face unto the Lord God, to seek by prayer and supplications, with fasting, and sackcloth, and ashes:

Daniel sets in to pray for his people.

4 And I prayed unto the Lord my God, and made my confession and said, "O Lord, the great and dreadful God, keeping the covenant and mercy to them that love Him, and to them that keep His commandments;

"You, God, are good."

5 "We have sinned, and have committed iniquity, and have done wickedly, and have rebelled, even by departing from Thy precepts and from Thy judgments:

6 "Neither have we hearkened unto Thy servants the prophets, which spake in Thy name to our kings, our princes, and our fathers and to all the people of the land.

"We have sinned big time."

7 "O Lord, righteousness belongeth unto Thee, but unto us confusion of faces, as at this day; to the men of Judah, and to the inhabitants of Jerusalem, and unto all Israel, that are near, and that are far off, through all the countries withther Thou hast driven them, because of their trespass that they have trespassed against Thee.

Daniel acknowledges that it is God who has scattered the Israelites throughout the whole known world.

8 "O Lord, to us belongeth confusion of face, to our kings, to our princes, and to our fathers, because we have sinned against Thee.

9 "To the Lord our God belong mercies and forgiveness, though we have rebelled against Him.

None of us deserve God's forgiveness.

10 "Neither have we obeyed the voice of the Lord our God, to walk in His laws, which He set before us by His servants the prophets.

11 "Yea, all Israel have transgressed Thy law, even by departing, that they might not obey Thy voice; therefore the curse is poured upon us, and the oath that is written in the law of Moses the servant of God, because we have sinned against Him.

12 "And He hath confirmed His words, which He spake against us and against our judges that judged us, by bringing upon us a great evil: for under the whole heaven hath not been done as hath been done upon Jerusalem.

God did just as He promised.

13 "As it is written in the Law of Moses, all this evil is come upon us: yet made we not our prayer before the Lord our God, that we might turn from our iniquities, and understand Thy truth.

And still Israel/Judah didn't repent.

14 "Therefore that the Lord watched upon the evil, and brought it upon us: for the Lord our God is righteous in all His works which He doeth: for we obeyed not His voice.

15 "And now, O Lord our God, Thou hast brought Thy people forth out of the land of Egypt with a mighty hand, and hast gotten Thee renown, as at this day: we have sinned, we have done wickedly.

"God, you rescued us from Egypt."

16 "O Lord, according to all Thy righteousness, I beseech Thee, let Thine anger and Thy fury be turned away from Thy city Jerusalem, Thy Holy Mountain: because for our sins, and for the iniquities of our fathers, Jerusalem and Thy people are become a reproach to all that are about us.

"Please quit being angry with us, though we don't deserve otherwise."

17 "Now therefore, O our God, hear the prayer of Thy servant, and his supplications, and cause Thy face to shift upon thy sanctuary that is desolate, for the Lord's sake.

"God, I know we have sinned and deserved to be punished, but please listen to me."

18 "O my God, incline Thine ear, and hear; open Thine eyes, and behold our desolations, and the city which is called by Thy name: for we do not present our supplications before Thee for our righteousness, but for Thy great mercies.

19 "O Lord, hear; O Lord, forgive: O Lord, hearken and do; defer not, for Thine Own sake, O my God: for Thy city and Thy people are called by Thy name."

"God You promised Jeremiah that You would return us to the city called by Your Name. You deserve no less than the glory for fulfilling that promise."

20 And while I was speaking and praying, and confessing my sin and the sin of my people Israel, and presenting my supplication before the Lord my God for the Holy Mountain of my God,

21 Yea, while I was speaking in prayer, even the man Gabriel, whom I had seen in the vision at the beginning, being caused to fly swiftly, touched me about the time of the evening oblation.

The same angel came to visit him that he had seen before.

22 And he informed me, and talked with me, and said, "O Daniel, I am now come forth to give thee skill and understanding.

23 "At the beginning of thy supplications the commandment came forth, and I am come to show thee; for thou art greatly beloved: therefore understand the matter, and consider the vision.

"God really loves you, so He is sending you a vision to explain things."

24 "Seventy weeks ...

A week means seven just as our word dozen means twelve. Nearly everyone agrees that this is talking about 490 years; 70x7 years.

... are determined upon thy people (Israel/Judah; God sees them as one people)

and upon thy holy city, to finish the transgression, (for Israel to end their sins)

and to make an end of sins, (their time is up)

and to make reconciliation for iniquity (Calvary)

and to bring in everlasting righteousness, (Jesus' work on Calvary) *and to seal up the vision and prophecy,* (to complete everything ever prophesied to the Jews)

and to anoint the most Holy (Jesus).

These six things are going to happen in the next 490 years; specifically, they were fulfilled in Christ.

This is a time line, a schedule. It must stay intact in order to mean anything. Otherwise it would be like breaking the end off of a ruler, stapling a piece of elastic onto both pieces and trying to measure something.

25 "Know therefore and understand, that from the going forth of the commandment ...

Given by Cyrus I in about 457 BC

...to restore and to build Jerusalem unto the Messiah the Prince...

Jesus

...shall be seven weeks, and threescore and two weeks...

[7x7]+[62x7]=483 years.

...the street shall be built again, and the wall, even in troublous times.

No kidding. Read Ezra and Nehemiah. This is the first 49 years.

26 And after (the) *threescore and two weeks shall Messiah be cut off* (crucified), *but not for himself* (for us):

Our system of dates (BC-AD) was set up by a monk in the 500's AD. He used the records of the Roman Empire to figure the dates backward and set the birth of Christ in year 1_{AD}. Unfortunately, he didn't realize that the 15th year of Tiberius mentioned in Luke included a 5 year co-reign with Augustus. This made his dates 5 years too late. Christ was born, then, in what we would call 5_{BC} (5 years "Before Christ").

and the people of the prince...

The prince is Titus, the general who led the armies against Jerusalem in AD 70. His father was appointed Emperor just beforehand. So "the people of the prince" are gentiles- Romans.

... that shall come shall destroy the city and the sanctuary; and the end thereof shall be with a flood, and unto the end of the war desolations are determined.

In $_{AD}$70 Titus destroyed Jerusalem with a flood of soldiers, made the city desolate, ended the greatest time of tribulation known to man, and the nation of Israel/Judah was no more.

27 And he

Christ

...shall confirm the covenant with many for one week

Seven years

...and in the midst of the week

After three and a half years of ministry

...he

Christ

...shall cause the sacrifice and the oblation to cease

We don't have to torch sheep anymore since The Cross.

...and for the overspreading of abominations

Abundance of sins

...He

Christ through Titus.

...shall make it

The city

...desolate, even until the consummation

Consummation is "The end or completion of the present system of things;" Noah Webster 1828 dictionary. So "He shall make the city desolate until the end of the present system."

...and that determined shall be poured upon the desolate

The Jews remaining in Jerusalem in AD 70.

Christ was born about 5_{BC}. This would make Christ thirty in 25 AD (483 years after Cyrus told the Jews to go back home- 457_{BC}), the age the Bible says He began His ministry. He preached for three and a half years and was crucified ("cut off in the midst of the week"). For some time after The Crucifixion no one but Jews were saved. I believe Cornelius (the first gentile) was saved three and a half years after The Crucifixion, completing the last "week" and ending the Jews 490 years since Cyrus' command to return. After this time the doors of salvation were permanently opened to everyone, no matter what their nationality. The Jew's time, the system of salvation by keeping the Mosaic Law, was permanently ended.

Chapter 10
DANIEL TALKS TO AN ANGEL

1 In the third year of Cyrus king of Persia a thing was revealed unto Daniel, whose name was called Belteshazzar; and the thing was true, but the time appointed was long: and he understood the thing, and had understanding of the vision.

This is about 455 BC.

2 In those days I Daniel was mourning three full weeks.

3 I ate no pleasant bread, neither came flesh nor wine in my mouth, neither did I anoint myself at all, till three whole weeks were fulfilled.

Daniel had his nation on his heart and was fasting about their future. He had the prophecies available to him from Isaiah and Jeremiah that said Israel would be in captivity for seventy years. That time is about up.

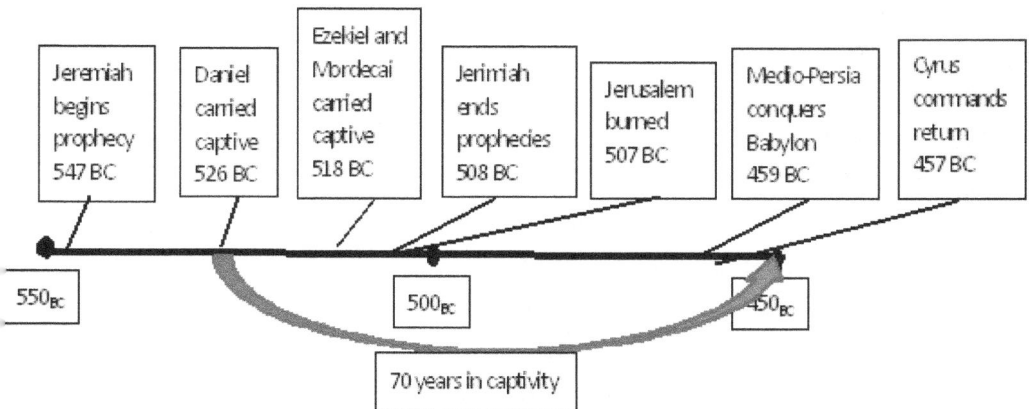

Note, it was special enough that he didn't drink wine during this time for it to mentioned as part of his fasting. Obviously, he drank wine the rest of the time.

4 And in the four and twentieth day of the first month, as I was by the side of the great river, which is Hiddekel;

The Hiddekel is probably the Tigris.

5 Then I lifted up mine eyes, and looked, and behold a certain man clothed in linen, whose loins were girded with fine gold of Uphaz:

6 His body also was like the beryl, and His face as the appearance of lightning, and His eyes as lamps of fire, and His arms and His feet like in color to polished brass, and the voice of His words like the voice of a multitude.

This description sounds a lot like other descriptions in Daniel and Revelations of God. Further verses make it sound like he is an angel, though.

7 And I Daniel alone saw the vision: for the men that were with me saw not the vision; but a great quaking fell upon them, so that they fled to hide themselves.

Earthquake or Devine fear?

8 Therefore I was left alone, and saw this great vision, and there remained no strength in me: for my comeliness was turned in me into corruption, and I retained no strength.

9 Yet heard I the voice of His words: and when I heard the voice of His words, then was I in a deep sleep on my face, and my face toward the ground.

10 And, behold, an hand touched me, which set me upon my knees and upon the palms of my hands.

11 And he said unto me, "O Daniel, a man greatly beloved, understand the words that I speak unto thee, and stand upright: for unto thee am I now sent." And when he had spoken this word unto me, I stood trembling.

12 Then said he unto me, "Fear not, Daniel: for from the first day that thou didst set thine heart to understand, and to chasten thyself before thy God, thy words were heard, and I am come for thy words.

13 "But the prince of the kingdom of Persia withstood me one and twenty days: but, lo, Michael, one of the chief princes, came to help me; and I remained there with the kings of Persia.

We don't know who this "prince of Persia" was. It is possible he was Cyrus or a spiritual being responsible for the area of Persia. There is no indication of how this "prince" withstood him nor how Michael helped him.

14 "Now I am come to make thee understand what shall befall thy people in the latter days: for yet the vision is for many days."

The angel strengthens Daniel.

15 And when he had spoken such words unto me, I set my face toward the ground, and I became dumb.

16 And, behold, one like the similitude of the sons of men touched my lips: then I opened my mouth, and spake, and said unto him that stood before me, "O my lord, by the vision my sorrows are turned upon me, and I have retained no strength.

The vision he saw is recorded in chapter 11.

17 "For how can the servant of this my Lord talk with this my lord? For as for me, straightway there remained no strength in me, neither is there breath left in me."

Daniel is so upset he can't stand up or hardly even breath.

18 Then there came again and touched me one like the appearance of a man, and he strengthened me,

19 And said, "O man greatly beloved, fear not: peace be unto thee, be strong, yea, be strong." And when he had spoken unto me, I was strengthened, and said, "Let my lord speak; for thou hast strengthened me."

Imagine being called by an angel "greatly beloved"? God had a special love for Daniel.

20 Then said he, "Knowest thou wherefore I come unto thee? And now will I return to fight with the prince of Persia: and when I am gone forth, lo, the prince of Grecia shall come."

The Prince of Persia might be the current king and the Prince of Greece Alexander the Great.

21 "But first I will tell you what is written in the Book of Truth. (No one supports me against them except Michael, your prince.

The word prince here means ruler. All in all, quite a confusing chapter. We still don't really know how to interpret most of it.

Chapter 11
THE COMING KINGS

1 Also I, in the first year of Darius the Mede, even I, stood to confirm and to strengthen him.

This is still the angel speaking to Daniel.

2 And now will I show thee the truth. Behold, there shall stand up yet three kings in Persia; and the fourth shall be far richer than they all: and by his strength through his riches he shall stir up all against the realm of Grecia.

Darius the Mede was likely Cyrus Uncle Father-in-Law. He was King of Mede and partnered with Cyrus to conquer the surrounding areas. Cyrus inherited the Median throne upon Darius' death.

(A note about dates: Secular, and sadly, most Christian historians use the dates given by Ptolemy in the second century AD as their basis for all ancient history. You will find all textbooks, Wikipedia, and even Bible footnotes based on these dates. Unfortunately, Ptolemy's dates contradict not just Biblical prophecy, but Jewish and Persian histories, and Josephus (1st century AD and history pulled from older sources not available to Ptolemy.)

For example, to fit the amount of time he gave the Persian Empire, Ptolemy says there were ten kings of Persia, while Josephus, who had access to the library of Alexandria, says there were only six (two before Cyrus). Persian and Hebrew tradition agrees more with Josephus.

Why would Ptolemy give so much time to Persia? He based his history on the work of Greek historians, who had written down Oral Traditions of the Persians (their enemies, by the way). Unfortunately, with all the language

75

differences, the Greeks didn't realize that "Artaxerxes" was not a name, but a title ("Worthy to be King"). So when they heard stories about "Ahasuerus, son of Darius" and Artaxerxes, son of Darius" they thought they were hearing about four different people instead of two. This caused them to record five Darius' when there were really only two, and even to invent a second Alexander in their own history, since Persian records say the first Persian king by the name Darius fought with Alexander of Greece, while they knew for a fact that Alexander the Great had fought with the last Persian Darius. All these doubling of kings greatly expanded the timeline for Persia.

Some use Solar Eclipse dates to support Ptolemy's timeline, but to do so they must assume the ancients didn't notice the effects of an extra fourth of a day every year. This seems rather a silly assumption. Wouldn't you notice if Christmas occurred in the winter when you were a kid, but in the spring when you were an adult? Humans have been aware of the extra fourth day/year just about since the Flood.

If we readjust the dates to match the Bible and Persian and Hebrew tradition, it all fits together perfectly. And after all, who would know what happened better? The men who lived the events and wrote them down themselves, or Ptolemy who lived 600 years later... or even us, who live some 2300 years later?!

Rulers of Persia

1. **Cyrus II the Great** (his grandpa was a Cyrus, but not a very powerful king) conquered Babylon and its territory in 459_{BC} (This is when Darius the Mede, his uncle, ruled Babylon under Cyrus, but he died shortly

thereafter, leaving Cyrus in charge of the whole thing.) Cyrus possibly only ruled about 3 years after the death of his uncle.

2. **Ahaserus** (Xerexs in Greek) was Artaxerxes I (known as "son of Darius") and was Esther's husband. His sister had married Cyrus. He murdered his brother-in-law and sent **Cambyses II**, his nephew and Jr ruler to Egypt to control an uprising. He died there.

3. **Gaumata** (possibly Hamedetha according to Jewish histories) was a noble man who didn't like the transition Cyrus and Ahaserus were making in the country towards Zoroastrisme (at this time in history a monotheistic religion similar to, possibly a corruption of, Judaism). He killed Ahaserus and took the kingdom, reestablishing Baal and Asherah worship. He ruled a very short time.

4. **Darius II the Great (or The Persian),** son of Hystaspes, married Ahaserus' (and Esther's?) daughter, returned the country to Zoroastrisme, and killed Gaumata. He would have been the king of Ezra and Nehemiah's time. He demanded Tribute of dirt and water from Greece. This is just picking a fight. He then killed Alexander the Great's father, causing Alexander to attack Persia. Darius the Persian was extremely rich.

5. **Artaxerxes V Bessus**, an usurper who murdered Darius and continued the resistance against Alexander the Great from 330–329. (Alexander killed him)

Mede

Persia

Ahaserus I

Cyrus I

Darius I the Mede *Princess* ———— **Cambyses I**

**Ahaserus II
(killed Cyrus I,
married Esther)** *Princess* ———— **Cyrus II the Great
(Co-ruled with
Darius I)**

**Cambyses II
(Died fighting in
Egypt)**

**Hameditha
(Took the
Kingdom to
restore Baal
Worship)**

Princess ———— **Darius II the Persian
(Son of a Nobleman,
killed Hameditha,
Picked a fight with
Greece)**

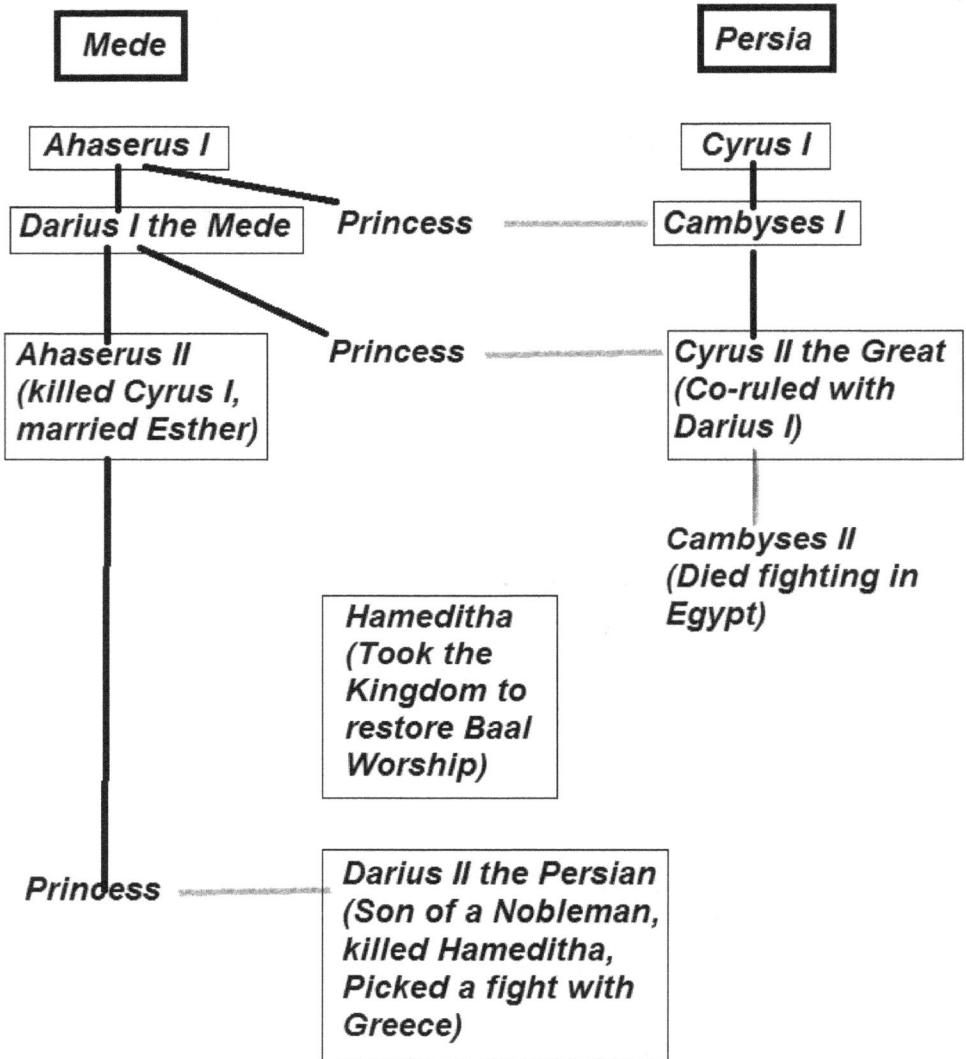

*...and the fourth shall be far richer than they all:
and by his strength through his riches he shall stir up
all against the realm of Grecia.*

The fourth king is called by the Greeks Xerxes I, but was likely Darius II The Persian (or The Great). Greek authors of the time tell us he was very rich. He had an army of at least 800,000 men making him very strong. He attacked Greece, but lost badly.

3 And a mighty king shall stand up, that shall rule with great dominion, and do according to his will.

Alexander has some of the greatest conquests in all of history. He took on the king of Persia and ruled over many countries. He was a total dictator.

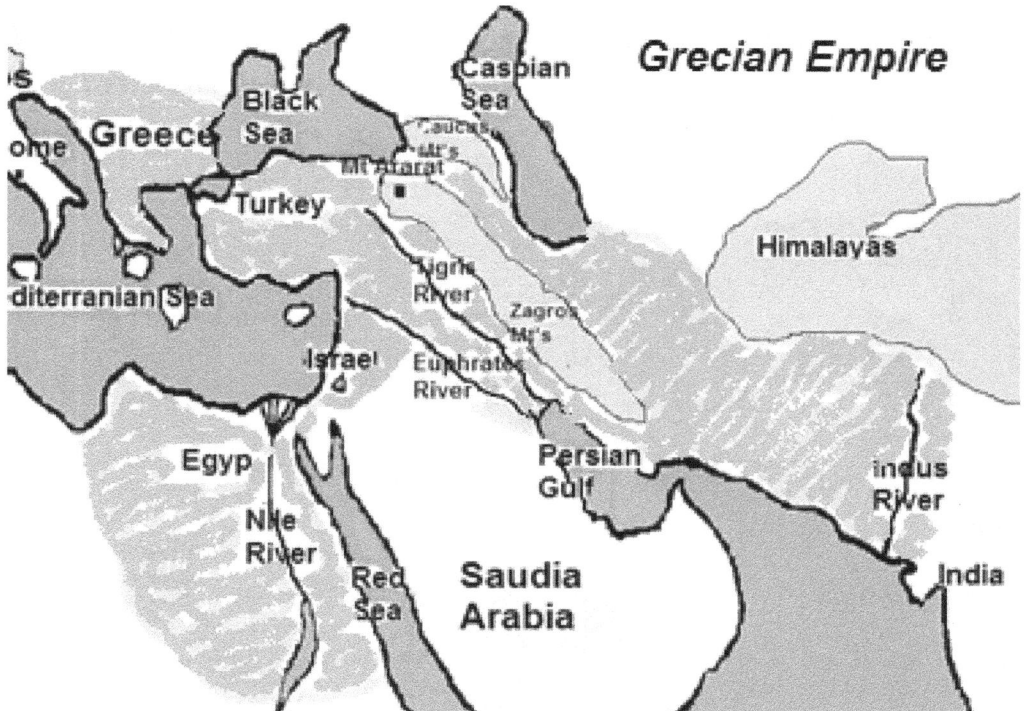

4 And when he shall stand up, his kingdom shall be broken, and shall be divided toward the four winds of heaven; and not to his posterity, nor according to

his dominion which he ruled: for his kingdom shall be plucked up, even for others beside those.

Alexander died at the height of his strength at the age of 32. His kingdom was divided into four parts, but not to his offspring. Arideus, his brother, was made king in Macedonia; Olympias, Alexander's mother, killed him, and poisoned Alexander's two sons, Hercules and Alexander. So his family was destroyed by its own hands. His generals finished off his mother.

Alexander's kingdom was then divided among his four generals.

5 And the king of the south shall be strong, and one of his princes ; and he (the prince) *shall be strong*

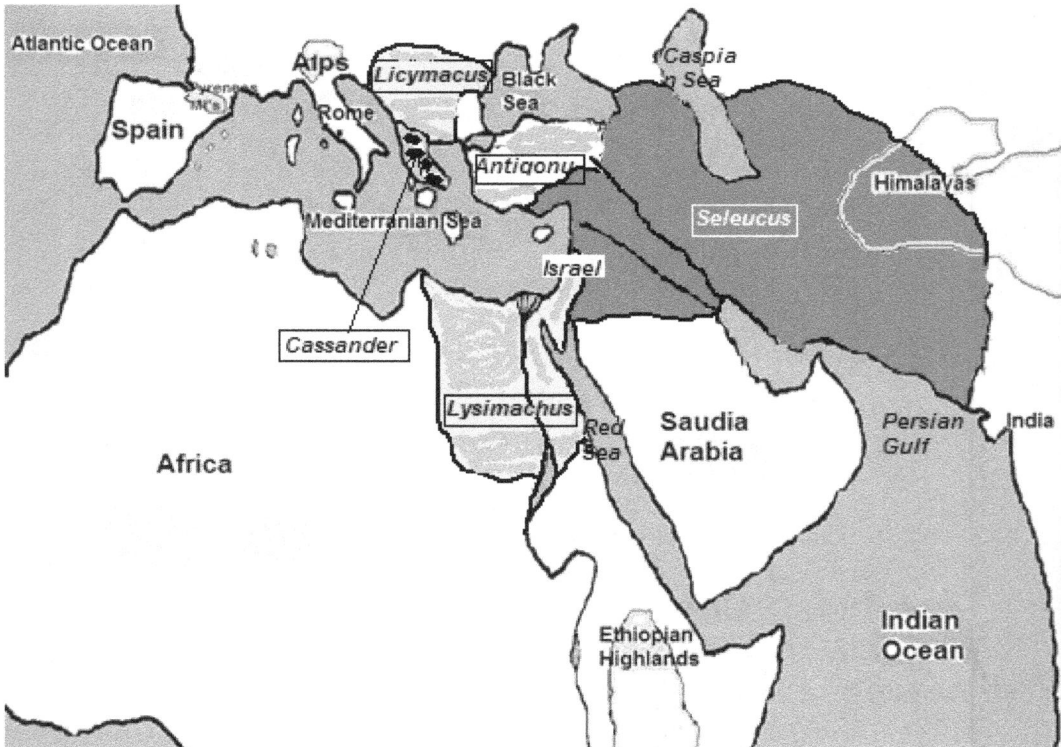

above him (the king of the south, Egypt), *and have dominion; his dominion shall be a great dominion.*

The kingdom of the south was ruled by one of Alexander's captains, Ptolemaeus Lagus, whose successors were called the Lagidae or Ptolemies. The countries that at first belonged to Ptolemy are Egypt, Phoenicia, Arabia, Libya, Ethiopia, and smaller tributaries.

The kingdom of Syria (called the kingdom of the north in these prophecies) was set up by Seleucus Nicanor, or "The Conqueror;" he was one of Ptolemy's princes or generals, and became stronger than Ptolemy, and had the largest territory of all. He was the most powerful of all Alexander's successors, ruling around seventy-two countries. Both these kingdoms (Egypt and Syria) gave Judah a great deal of trouble, especially since it was exactly between their two capitals. Ptolemy, soon after he gained Egypt, invaded Judea, and took Jerusalem on a Sabbath while pretending to make a friendly visit.

6 And in the end of years they shall join themselves together; for the king's daughter (Bernice) **of the south** (Egypt) **shall come to the king of the north** (Syria) **to make an agreement** (marriage)**: but she** (Bernice) **shall not retain the power of the arm** (the throne)**; neither shall he** (Antiochus king of Syria) **stand, nor his arm: but she shall be given up** (murdered)**, and they that brought her, and he that begat her, and he that strengthened her in these times** (they all died)**.**

About seventy years after Alexander's death, the King of Egypt and the Seleucidae of Syria pretended to try to unite. Ptolemy Philadelphus, king of Egypt, gave his daughter Bernice to Antiochus Theos, king of Syria, for a wife. Unfortunately, he divorced his first wife, Laodice, to enter this agreement. The whole deal fell apart.

Antiochus divorced Bernice and remarried Laodice, who soon poisoned him, had Bernice and her son murdered, and set up her own son by Antiochus, who was called Seleucus Callinicus, to be king.

7 But out of a branch of her (Bernice's) ***roots***(her brother) ***shall one stand up in his estate, which shall come with an army, and shall enter into the fortress of the king of the north*** (Syria)***, and shall deal against them, and shall prevail:***

8 And shall also carry captives into Egypt their gods, with their princes, and with their precious vessels of silver and of gold; and he shall continue more years than the king of the north.

9 So the king of the south shall come into his kingdom, and shall return into his own land.

Ptolemaeus Euergetes, the son and successor of Ptolemaeus Philadelphus (and brother to Bernice, thus "her branch"), came with an army against Seleucus Callinicus (son of Laodice and Antiochus Theos), king of Syria, to avenge his sister, and won.

He carried away both people and riches into Egypt. This Ptolemy reigned forty-six years; if his problems at home had not called him away, Ptolemy would probably have conquered all of Syria. But he was forced to go home to Egypt to keep control there

10 But his (Seleucus Callinicus of Syria) ***sons shall be stirred up, and shall assemble a multitude of great forces: and one shall certainly come, and overflow, and pass through: then shall he return, and be stirred up, even to his fortress.***

Seleucus Callinicus, who died miserably, left two sons, Seleucus and Antiochus; these are his sons that "shall be stirred up, and shall assemble a multitude of great forces," to recover what their father had lost.

But the older son, Seleucus, was weak and unable to rule his army, and was poisoned by his friends. He reigned only two years.

His brother Antiochus III succeeded him. He reigned thirty-seven years, and was called "The Great." That is why the angel speaks of sons at first, but then goes on with the account of one son, who was only fifteen years old when he began to reign. He certainly "came, and overflowed, and over-ran," and restored what his father had lost.

11 And the king of the south (Egypt) **shall be moved with choler** (anger)**, and shall come forth and fight with him** (Antiochus III)**, even with the king of the north** (Syria)**: and he** (Ptolemaeus Philopater,) **shall set forth a great multitude; but the multitude shall be given into his** (Ptolemaeus Philopater) **hand.**

Ptolemaeus Philopater got very mad and beat Antiochus III at first. He had 70,000 foot soldiers, 5000 horsemen, and seventy-three elephants. And the other "multitude" (the army of Antiochus, consisting of 62,000 foot soldiers, 6000 horsemen, and 102 elephants) lost.

12 And when he (Ptolemaeus) **hath taken away the multitude, his heart shall be lifted up; and he shall cast down many ten thousands: but he shall not be strengthened by it.**

Ptolemaeus' victory went to his head. He went into the temple of God at Jerusalem, and entered the Most Holy Place (which only the High Priest was supposed to do), which made God mad at him. Though he defeated a large army, it wasn't enough to protect him from God's anger.

13 For the king of the north shall return, and shall set forth a multitude greater than the former, and shall certainly come after certain years with a great army and with much riches.

14 And in those times there shall many stand up against the king of the south:

The king of the north, Antiochus III the Great, rebuilt his army bigger than before and confronted Egypt again.

Meanwhile, Ptolemaeus Philopater had died leaving Ptolemaeus Epiphanes king, though he was still a child. This gave the advantage to Antiochus III the Great, who had made a treaty with the King of Macedon and Scopas his general, whom he sent into Syria. Antiochus defeated Ptolemaeus and destroyed a good deal of his army. The Jews willingly helped Antiochus besiege Ptolemaeus's garrisons in Judah, at this point viewing Egypt as the oppressor and Syria as the liberator.

15 So the king of the north (Antiochus) *shall come, and cast up a mount, and take the most fenced cities: and the arms of the south shall not withstand, neither his chosen people, neither shall there be any strength to withstand.*

16 But he (Antiochus) *that cometh against him* (Ptolomey) *shall do according to his own will, and none shall stand before him* (Antiochus)*: and he* (Antiochus) *shall stand in the glorious land* (Israel), *which by his hand shall be consumed.*

Antiochus the Great surprised Egypt and all the power of the king of Egypt, couldn't stop him. He also conquered the land of Judea/Israel which is "The Glorious Land" and flattened it. He fed his army with all the food of the land.

Judea lay between Egypt and Syria, so in all the wars between the two, Israel suffered.

17 He (Antiochus) **shall also set his face to enter with the strength of his whole kingdom, and upright ones** (Israelites) **with him; thus shall he do: and he** (The King of Egypt) **shall give him the daughter of women, corrupting her: but she shall not stand on his** (her father's) **side, neither be for him.**

The King of Egypt gave Antiochus one of the early Cleopatras (there were around ten, total, in history. The famous one was the last one.) as a wife in hopes it would cause him problems, but she ended up siding with her husband instead of her father, so it didn't work.

18 After this shall he (Antiochus) **turn his face unto the isles of the sea** (owned by Rome) **and shall take many: but a prince** (Generals Scipio of Rome) **for his own behalf shall cause the reproach offered by him** (Antiochus) **to cease; without his own reproach he shall cause it to turn upon him.**

Antiochus III the Great started a war with Rome (at this time still a republic, though growing in power.) He took many of the islands about the Hellespont- Rhodes, Samos, Delos, etc. But the two Scipios (Roman generals) were sent with an army against him. Hannibal was with Antiochus and advised him to invade Italy and loot it as he had done (the famous "Elephant-over-the-Alps" move); but Antiochus did not take his advice, though he did use elephants in his army, unfortunately, since at the most crucial moment in battle several panicked and trampled his own troops. The Scipio brothers ("prince" means "ruler" and applies to generals as well as royalty) battled with him, and whipped him bad, though Antiochus had 70,000 men and the Romans only 30,000.

19 Then he (Antiochus) **shall turn his face toward the fort of his own land but he shall stumble and fall, and not be found.**

When Antiochus lost to the Romans, and was forced to give up all he had in Europe, and had a very heavy tax laid on him, he went home and plundered a temple of Jupiter to get the money to pay his taxes. This so angered his own people that they killed him. And so he was "not to be found."

20 Then shall stand up in his estate a raiser of taxes in the glory of the kingdom: but within few days he shall be destroyed, neither in anger, nor in battle.

Seleucus Philopater, the elder son of Antiochus the Great, oppressed his own people, and imposed very high taxes. When he was told he would lose his friends because of it, he said he knew no better friend he had than money.

He also tried to rob the temple at Jerusalem.

He was poisoned by Heliodorus, his general and tax collector, when he had reigned only twelve years, and done nothing else remarkable.

Now we begin the prophecy of the reign of Antiochus IV Epiphanes, the little horn spoken of before (chapter 8:9) who was a sworn enemy to the Jewish religion.

21 And in his (Antiochus III the Great) **estate shall stand up a vile person** (Antiochus IV Epiphanes)**, to whom they shall not give the honor of the kingdom:**

but he shall come in peaceably, and obtain the kingdom by flatteries.

Antiochus IV called himself Epiphanes (The Illustrious). He was a horrid person. Non-Jewish writers describe him to be an odd-humored man, rude and boisterous, base and sordid. He would sometimes disguise himself, sneak out of the court into the city, and roam with any low class company he could find. He had the most unaccountable whims. A real nutcase. Some called him Epimanes (the madman).

He had been held a hostage at Rome for a long time to buy the faithfulness of his father when the Romans had conquered him. It was agreed that, when the other hostages were exchanged, he should continue a prisoner-at-large.

22 And with the arms of a flood shall the enemies be overflown from before him (Antiochus IV Epiphanes)***, and shall be broken; yea, also the prince of the covenant*** (Antiochus IV Epiphanes' nephew)***.***

23 And after the league made with him he shall work deceitfully: for he shall come up, and shall become strong with a small people.

Antiochus IV arranged to have his older brother's son, Demetrius, be sent a hostage to Rome, in exchange for himself. Since his older brother was killed by his general, Heliodorus the Tax Collector (verse 20), Antiochus IV took the kingdom.

He came to the throne peaceably pretending to reign for his nephew.

The Syrians didn't give him the throne nor did he take it in war. Two neighboring princes, Eumenes and Attalus, helped him gain popularity with the people. He flattered others until they all preferred him over his nephew. Then he took care of his brother's murderer Heliodorus, who tried to rebel against him with a large army. Those that opposed Antiochus were destroyed, even his nephew, the rightful heir ("prince of the covenant").

24 He shall enter peaceably even upon the fattest places of the province; and he shall do that which his fathers have not done, nor his fathers' fathers; he shall scatter among them the prey, and spoil, and riches: yea, and he shall forecast his devices against the strong holds, even for a time.

Antiochus IV gave the common people lots of money; shared the loot from war to make them like him. No other Syrian king had done anything like this. But while he was doing this, he was putting into place what he needed to hold the throne after he quit being generous. Once he had the kingdom firmly in his control, he began ruling with an iron hand.

25 And he (Antiochus IV) *shall stir up his power and his courage against the king of the south* (Egypt) *with a great army; and the king of the south shall be stirred up to battle with a very great and mighty army; but he* (Ptolemy of Egypt) *shall not stand: for they* (his own generals) *shall forecast devices against him.*

He went to war with Ptolemaeus Philometer, king of Egypt. Ptolemy fought back with a very large army;

26 Yea, they that feed of the portion of his (Ptolemy's) *meat shall destroy him, and his* (Antiochus's) *army shall overflow: and many shall fall down slain.*

Ptolemy, though he has such a vast army, wasn't able to defeat him. Antiochus's army slaughtered the Egyptians. Ptolemy's counselors, who ate at his own table, were bribed by Antiochus IV.

27 And both of these kings' hearts shall be to do mischief, and they shall speak lies at one table; but it shall not prosper: for yet the end shall be at the time appointed.

After the battle, these two kings met to make a peace treaty, but neither one intended to keep any part of it. God appointed a time for the war to resume.

28 Then shall he (Antiochus) **return into his land with great riches; and his heart shall be against the holy covenant; and he shall do exploits, and return to his own land.**

He looted Jerusalem (and in fact, all of Israel) on the way home. He enjoyed torturing them.

29 At the time appointed he shall return, and come toward the south; but it shall not be as the former, or as the latter.

Again, Antiochus attacked Egypt. He had brought home a great deal of loot from his last war there, and this made him very eager to attack again. Two years later, in the eighth year of his reign, he attacked but this time he didn't succeed.

30 For the ships of Chittim shall come against him: therefore he shall be grieved, and return, and have indignation against the holy covenant: so shall he do; he shall even return, and have intelligence with them that forsake the holy covenant.

"The ships of Chittim" are the Roman navy with ambassadors from the Roman Senate. Ptolemaeus

Philometer, king of Egypt, made a deal with the Romans and received their help against Antiochus. The Syrians had besieged Ptolemy and his mother, a Cleopatra, in the city of Alexandria. The Roman senate sent an embassy to Antiochus and commanded him to stop the siege. He asked for time to consider it. Popilius, one of the ambassadors, drew a circle around him, and told him he had to give a positive answer before he came out of the circle. Fearing the Roman power, he was forced to give orders for the retreat of his army out of Egypt.

This made him mad.

In his return from Egypt, he always stopped by Israel and tormented them, spoiling the city and temple. But the worst attack was in his return from Egypt after meeting with Rome. Because he couldn't win in Egypt, he took his revenge out on the Jews, who hadn't provoked him, but who had provoked God. That was why He allowed it.

31 And arms shall stand on his part, and they (the Syrians) *shall pollute the sanctuary of strength, and shall take away the daily sacrifice, and they shall place the abomination that maketh desolate.*

Antiochus IV already had a hatred of the Jews' religion. He hated the Law of Moses and the worship of the true God, and was irritated at the privileges of the Jewish nation and the promises made to them by God.

Antiochus not only destroyed the city and ransacked the temple, he placed an idol in it and sacrificed pigs to it.

32 And such as do wickedly against the covenant (unbelieving Jews) *shall he corrupt by flatteries: but the people that do know their God shall be strong, and do exploits.*

33 And they that understand among the people shall instruct many: yet they shall fall by the sword, and by flame, by captivity, and by spoil, many days.

Antiochus was helped by some apostate Jews who spied for him and introduced the foreign customs.

1 Maccabees 1:11 to 15 records that those back-slidden Jews "made themselves uncircumcised and forsook the holy covenant."

2 Maccabees 4:9 tells of Jason, the brother of Onias the high priest, who, under Antiochus' command, set up a school at Jerusalem, for the training up of the children in the fashions of the heathen (much like our public schools do today).

2 Maccabees 4:23 and other places tell of Menelaus who helped Antiochus into Jerusalem.

The Maccabees tell us a lot about the damage done to the believing Jews by these traitors. Antiochus IV used them all he could to get the people to turn their backs on God. He flattered them and used them as decoys to draw others away. Antiochus not only used his own army, but many who had turned their backs on God. They helped him take away the golden alter and candlesticks and anything else of value.

Antiochus went into the Holiest of Holies (the place only the High Priest was ever allowed, and then only once a year), Menelaus the traitor guiding him. He had decided to make all the Jews convert to his religion, so he took away the daily sacrifice and set up the "Abomination of Desolation" on the altar (An idol- 1 Maccabees 1:54), and called The Temple "The Temple Of Jupiter Olympius," (2 Maccabees 6:2). Many converted and he persecuted those who wouldn't.

The "exploits" mentioned are the things done by those who resisted. Even Antiochus became ashamed of what he was doing, he treated them so horribly.

One of the principle scribes, Eleazar, had pig meat forced into his mouth. He spit it out knowing he would be tortured to death for doing it. Many chose to be put to death instead of denying God. They were tortured, "not accepting deliverance," as it says in Hebrews 11:35. "Exploits" also refers to the military courage and achievements of Judas Maccabaeus and others in opposition to Antiochus.

We are told in verse 33 that these people who would not deny God would instruct many, and they did. They made it their business to show others what they had learned themselves of the difference between truth and falsehood, good and evil.

34 Now when they (the righteous) **shall fall, they shall be holpen with a little help: but many shall cleave to them with flatteries.**

They fell by the cruelty of Antiochus IV. He was so angry he tortured any of them he could catch to death. The Maccabees tell us he slew in wars and murdered in cold blood. Women were put to death for having their children circumcised, and their babies were hanged, among many other atrocities (1 Maccabees 1:60, 61).

35 And some of them of understanding shall fall, to try them, and to purge, and to make them white, even to the time of the end: because it is yet for a time appointed.

But why did God allow this? How can this be reconciled with the justice and goodness of God? It makes more sense if we consider what it was that God was aiming for; has always aimed for.

Even the best among us have flaws that need to be fixed. Some of those who understood the Word were tortured and killed in order to purify them and the church as a whole. This was God's way of weaning them from the world, and awakening them to greater seriousness and diligence in religion. Their sufferings for righteousness' sake tried and purged the nation of the Jews of their falseness, convinced them of the truth and power of the religion which these understanding men died for. It prepared them for the coming of the Messiah just a century and a half later. The blood of these martyrs was the seed of The Church.

But they weren't completely run down. They were given a little help. Judas Maccabaeus, and his brothers, and a few others did have some success against the tyrant. They pulled down the idolatrous altars, circumcised the children that they found uncircumcised, rescued The Law out of the hand of the Gentiles, (1 Maccabees 2:45, etc.)

Verse 35 also says "many shall cleave to them with flatteries." Some Jews joined the Maccabees when they saw them beginning to win, though they were not religious. They pretended friendship to either betray them or in hopes of "ridding their coat tails" so to speak. But the fiery trial separated between the true believers and the pretenders.

Though these troubles may continue a long time, they had an appointed end fixed in the plans of God.

36 And the king shall do according to his will; and he shall exalt himself, and magnify himself above

every god, and shall speak marvelous things against the God of gods, and shall prosper till the indignation be accomplished: for that that is determined shall be done.

This was fulfilled when Antiochus forbade sacrifices to be offered in God's temple, and ordered the Sabbaths to be profaned, and the sanctuary to be polluted (1 Maccabees 1:45).

Antiochus wrote to his own kingdom that everyone should leave the gods they had worshipped for generations, and worship the ones he had chosen. No one had ever done such a thing before. The heathens agreed because, though they liked their gods, they didn't like them enough to suffer for them. And, anyway, an idol is an idol. He wasn't really asking them to make that big of a change.

Antiochus was so proud that he thought he was above mortal man, that he could command the waves of the sea, and reach to the stars of heaven, as his insolence and haughtiness are expressed in 2 Maccabees 9:8, 10.

36 Till he had run his length, and filled up the measure of his iniquity; for that which is determined shall be done, and nothing more, nothing short.

37 Neither shall he regard the God of his fathers, nor the desire of women, nor regard any god: for he shall magnify himself above all.

People have a desire to worship the gods of their ancestors as much as they desire sex. It is unnatural to change gods. ("for, if you search through the isles of Chittim, you will not find an instance of a nation that has changed its gods," Jeremiah 2:10, 11). Yet Antiochus made laws to abolish the religion of his country, and brought in the idols of the Greeks. And though his predecessors had honored the God of Israel, and given great gifts to the temple at Jerusalem (2 Maccabees 3:2, 3), Antiochus IV insulted God and His temple in the greatest way possibly.

His not "regarding the desire of women" may mean his cruelty was so extreme he spared neither women nor children. Or it may mean he was homosexual, or it may refer to his contempt of everything normal men honor. Doesn't matter, since Antiochus IV fulfilled them all.

38 But in his estate shall he honor the god of forces: and a god whom his fathers knew not shall he honor with gold, and silver, and with precious stones, and pleasant things.

His ancestors worshiped the gods of pleasure, Apollo and Diana. Instead he worshiped the god of war and force, Jupiter Olympius, known about the Phoenicians as Baal-Semen. He set up an image of Jupiter in the temple at Jerusalem and offered gold, silver, jewels and pigs to it.

39 Thus shall he do in the most strong holds with a strange god, whom he shall acknowledge and increase with glory: and he shall cause them to rule over many, and shall divide the land for gain.

Antiochus IV committed Jerusalem to Jupiter instead of the true God and brought the idol a great deal of glory. He put the priests of Jupiter in charge of the country and they used the land for their own profit. He and they worshipped money, as most unbelievers do.

40 And at the time of the end shall the king of the south push at him: and the king of the north shall

come against him like a whirlwind, with chariots, and with horsemen, and with many ships; and he shall enter into the countries, and shall overflow and pass over.

This scripture had to have been fulfilled before the invention of the combustible engine. Armies have not used chariots and horsemen since and would not return to their use now.

41 He shall enter also into the glorious land, and many countries shall be overthrown: but these shall escape out of his hand, even Edom, and Moab, and the chief of the children of Ammon.

42 He shall stretch forth his hand also upon the countries: and the land of Egypt shall not escape.

43 But he shall have power over the treasures of gold and of silver, and over all the precious things of Egypt: and the Libyans and the Ethiopians shall be at his steps.

Antiochus IV had yet another war with Egypt. The Romans had kept him from invading Ptolemy, but now the king of Egypt attacked him and tried to take some of his territories. Antiochus IV fought back with chariots, and horses, and many ships; a great army. In this flying march many countries were overthrown by him, and he entered the land of Israel again.

He destroyed many of the neighboring countries, though some escaped such as Edom and Moab, and most of the children of Ammon. He didn't tax these people because they had helped him conquer Israel.

He stripped Egypt so bare that he permanently impoverished it. This was his fourth and final war with Egypt. He was pretending to help the younger brother of

Ptolemaeus Philometer against his brother. We don't read of any great slaughters at this time, but he thoroughly plundered everyone. He evidently threw a big party with all this money. He also got the Lybians and Ethiopians to serve him and help him against Egypt.

44 But tidings out of the east and out of the north shall trouble him: therefore he shall go forth with great fury to destroy, and utterly to make away many.

45 And he shall plant the tabernacles of his palace between the seas in the glorious holy mountain; yet he shall come to his end, and none shall help him.

This predicts Antiochus' fall, just like Daniel 8:25. He received word from the north-east parts of his kingdom that the king of Parthia was invading. This made him to drop what he was doing and go take care of the Persians and Parthians that were revolting against him. This irritated him because he had meant to totally ruin and destroy the Jews. We read in 1 Maccabees. 3:27, etc., that he was in a great rage when he heard of the successes of Judas Maccabaeus, and he gave orders to destroy Jerusalem. Then he pitched tents of his court between the Great Sea and the Dead Sea, setting up his royal pavilion at Emmaus near Jerusalem to show that, though he wasn't there, he had given full power to his officers to fight the Jews.

God cut him off in the height of his strength. No one could stop Him. This was also foretold in chapter 8:25 ("He shall be broken without hand"). As we discussed there, he came down with a horrid disease of the bowls where he essentially rotted from the inside out.

Nothing is prophesied about the kings after Antiochus IV. He was the most evil enemy of the church. In fact, Rome soon became a major player in the area causing a weakening of Syria.

Chapter 12
THE END OF THE MATTER

1 And at that time shall Michael stand up, the great prince which standeth for the children of thy people:...

"At that time" means at the end of that time, or shortly after these events. Michael (Michael = "who is like God"- Strong's Concordance) otherwise known as Jesus, appeared as His church's protector. Though Syria no longer had the power to persecute the Jews, from this time on they had to deal with Rome and its many campaigns in the area. Also, this is the time the Pharisees came to power. They persecuted anyone who truly believed God instead of them. Christ is that Great Prince, the King of Kings. He stood up for our salvation and still stands as an intercessor for us today.

...and there shall be a time of trouble, such as never was since there was a nation even to that same time: ...

This is the destruction of Jerusalem in AD 70, which Christ refers to in Matthew 24. This event resulted in women eating their own children because the hunger was so bad.

... thy people shall be delivered, every one that shall be found written in the book.

"Thy People" are those that love God as much as Daniel does. We are delivered through Calvary; all of us that are written in the Lamb's Book of Life.

Also, those that listened to Christ and sermon on the Mount of Olives knew to leave the Jerusalem and were spared the great persecution of that time.

2 And many of them that sleep in the dust of the earth shall awake, some to everlasting life, and some to shame and everlasting contempt.

3 And they that be wise shall shine as the brightness of the firmament; and they that turn many to righteousness as the stars forever and ever.

Ezekiel, in chapter 37, compares Israel's return from Babylon to a resurrection of dry bones. Here, it means resurrection to salvation, the Second Birth.

Those "resurrected to everlasting life" are the many Jews that accepted Christ in the first decade or so of the Church Age; those wise enough to recognize Messiah and teach others about Him.

Those resurrected to shame and contempt are those that rejected Christ.

4 But thou, O Daniel, shut up the words, and seal the book, even to the time of the end (of the Jewish nation; the subject of all these prophecies): *many shall run to and fro, and knowledge shall be increased.*

This prophecy wouldn't be understood or of much use to those alive in Daniel's time so he was told to seal it up for the future. It would be about 200 years until these writings would help anyone. At that time they were opened and searched for knowledge and help. They were a great comfort to those in Antiochus IV's time, and many people began to read the other parts of the Bible, learning about God. There were many who were expecting Christ at the proper time because of these prophecies of Daniel. In fact, anyone who wanted to do the math knew it was time for Jesus, since he was baptized 483 years (69 "weeks") after Cyrus gave the command to go back to Jerusalem.

5 Then I, Daniel, looked, and, behold, there stood other two, the one on this side of the bank of the river, and the other on that side of the bank of the river.

6 And one said to the man clothed in linen, which was upon the waters of the river, "How long shall it be to the end of these wonders?"

7 And I heard the man clothed in linen, which was upon the waters of the river, when he held up his right hand and his left hand unto heaven, and sware by him that liveth for ever that it shall be for a time, times, and an half;

A time here is a year, so this is a year, two years, and half a year. Josephus tells us in his "Book of the Wars of the Jews," that Antiochus IV Epiphanes surprised Jerusalem by force, and held it three and a half years, and then had to leave, his army.

8 And when he shall have accomplished to scatter the power of the holy people, all these things (prophesies) *shall be finished* (fulfilled).

God allowed Antiochus IV to win until he had scattered the power of Israel. God would allow him to do his worst and then Israel's time of punishment and refinement is done.

9 And I heard, but I understood not: then said I, "O my Lord, what shall be the end of these things?"

10 And he said, "Go thy way, Daniel: for the words are closed up and sealed till the time of the end (of the time of the Jews, the time these writings will be needed).

101

11 Many shall be purified, and made white, and tried; but the wicked shall do wickedly: and none of the wicked shall understand; but the wise shall understand.

12 And from the time that the daily sacrifice shall be taken away, and the abomination that maketh desolate set up, there shall be a thousand two hundred and ninety days. Blessed is he that waiteth, and cometh to the thousand three hundred and five and thirty days .

From the time Antiochus entered the city until the end of his rule over the city was 1290 days, or three years and seven months. This is when Antiochus left to fight in the north-east and the idol was destroyed, the temple cleansed and the sacrifices resumed. This is the event that was being celebrated in John 10:22, the Feast of (Re) Dedication.

It is believed Antiochus died about forty-five days after leaving Jerusalem, or 1335 days after he profaned the temple.

13 But go thou thy way till the end be: for thou shalt rest, and stand in thy lot at the end of the days.

"Don't you worry about all this Daniel. You will die before it happens and will stand before God on judgment day."

Conclusion

Many take verses out of Daniel to prove the futurist/dispensationalist interpretation of prophecy. In order to do this they must take a few verses here and put them with a few verses elsewhere that were never meant to go together.

The whole book of Daniel speaks of the end of the Israelite time frame, the Old Covenant; from the Babylonian captivity to AD 70. I have shown the historical fulfillment of each scripture.

If you wrote me a letter telling me you would give me $20 and then you gave me $20, it would not be right for my children to come to you twenty years from now and demand another $20. Yet this is just what the futurist view does. All these promises to Israel were fulfilled by $_{AD}$70.

The covenant with Israel was a conditional covenant. God only agreed to favor Israel as long as they worshiped Him as their God; as long as she was a faithful wife. Israel repeatedly rejected God and He divorced her (Jeremiah 3:8, Isaiah 50:1, Jeremiah 3:1, Hosea 2:2.) He then betrothed Himself to the Christian Church at Calvary, ushering in His Kingdom (Revelations 21:2, 9, Matthew 22:2-9, Matthew 25,).

It would be a violation of His own scripture for God to go back to His first "wife" (Duet 24:3-4). It simply does not make sense for God to go backwards. His relationship with Israel, the temple and sacrifices, etc., was a shadow of the coming Church Age and our personal relationship with Jesus.

Why would God go back to shadows when we now have the real thing? What would be the point?

This does not mean we won't face persecutions. Paul assured us we would. It simply means these exact persecutions talked about in Daniel won't happen again. They are done.

We can learn from them how to prevent God's judgment on our society and us personally and how to handle persecutions when they do come. We cannot use them to predict the future, though, since they have already been fulfilled.

Anything you read referencing "seven years," the abomination of desolation," "a country to the north attacking Israel," or anything else mentioned in Daniel has already happened, either at the time of Antiochus, the time of Christ, or AD 70. The scripture makes no mention of a second fulfilling of these same events. There is no reason to believe that they will happen again. To put them in the future or to say they will happen again is not dividing the Word of God correctly.

Why does it matter? When we Christians keep telling everyone that the "great seven year tribulation" spoken of in the Bible is coming, (such as when a new war starts in the Middle East) and then it doesn't happen, our word, and by extension, the Word of God is made to look like fools and totally unreliable.

Just since I have been an adult there have been at least a dozen different events that triggered "The sky is falling" type hysteria among the Christians.

Brothers and Sisters, the world is laughing at us! The fact is that if we show the prophecies given in the 500's BC and then show the fulfillment of those same scriptures in the 300's BC, AD 30's, and AD 70, then we show the prophecies that are still ahead of us, our words carry much more weight. It is important that we get this right. Other people's salvation depends on it.

BettySue

www.ingramcontent.com/pod-product-compliance
Lightning Source LLC
Chambersburg PA
CBHW022307060426
42446CB00007BA/743